Creative Flowdreaming™

ALSO BY SUMMER MCSTRAVICK

Flowdreaming: A Radical New Technique for Manifesting Anything You Want (book-with-CD)*

Flowdreaming for Enhanced Creativity and Success (audio CD)

Flowdreaming for Happy Relationships (audio CD)

Flowdreaming for Immediate Relief (audio CD)

Flowdreaming for Lots of Money, a Great Job, and a Luxury Lifestyle (audio CD)

Flowdreaming for Perfect Mental and Physical Health (audio CD)

Flowdreaming for Spiritual Progress (audio CD)

The Flowdreaming Prosperity Challenge (book-with-2-CD set)

God Is Always Happy, with Venus Andrecht (2-CD set)

*Available from Hay House

Please visit Hay House USA: **www.hayhouse.com**®
Hay House Australia: **www.hayhouse.com.au**
Hay House UK: **www.hayhouse.co.uk**
Hay House South Africa: **www.hayhouse.co.za**
Hay House India: **www.hayhouse.co.in**

Creative Flowdreaming™

Manifesting Your Dreams in the Life You've Already Got

Summer McStravick

HAY HOUSE, INC.
Carlsbad, California • New York City
London • Sydney • Johannesburg
Vancouver • Hong Kong • New Delhi

Published and distributed in the United States by: Hay House, Inc.: www.hayhouse.com • *Published and distributed in Australia by:* Hay House Australia Pty. Ltd.: www.hayhouse.com.au • *Published and distributed in the United Kingdom by:* Hay House UK, Ltd.: www.hayhouse.co.uk • *Published and distributed in the Republic of South Africa by:* Hay House SA (Pty), Ltd.: www.hayhouse.co.za • *Distributed in Canada by:* Raincoast: www.raincoast.com • *Published in India by:* Hay House Publishers India: www.hayhouse.co.in

Design: Riann Bender

Library of Congress Cataloging-in-Publication Data

McStravick, Summer.
  Creative flowdreaming : manifesting your dreams in the life you've already
    got / Summer McStravick. -- 1st ed.
      p. cm.
  ISBN 978-1-4019-2023-4 (tradepaper : alk. paper) 1. Success--Psychological
aspects. 2. Affirmations. I. Title.
  BF637.S8M3667 2009
  131--dc22   2008043427

ISBN: 978-1-4019-2023-4

12 11 10 09   4 3 2 1
1st edition, March 2009

Printed in the United States of America

*To my mother, Venus Andrecht, whose influence on my
thinking can be seen throughout this book and my life.
In particular, her connection with the Beings opened doors
to my thinking, it is the basis of much of the material
in this book, and it helped me make sense of the
new insights I have been exposed to.*

*I also offer this book to all those who are seeking a new direc-
tion and who are unafraid of what they will find there.*

Contents

Introduction

Lately, I've come to see myself as something of a manifesting practitioner. I suppose this is how many disciplines evolve: with someone waking up one day to discover that they've created something wholly different—or at least a unique variation on an old theme—then realizing that others are fascinated by their findings, so they begin to teach.

I've found a set of tools that works for me, and a cohesive perspective about living that seems to answer many of my questions, but which is still incomplete. Within this perspective lies a very spectacular truth: that you can learn to shape the subtle energies of your life, and thereby become a person with the ability to perform the magic of manifesting, or of guiding the woof and weave of the subtle energies that develop your future. But the ability to direct these energies is almost a side effect—a lesser truth—that pales against a larger understanding of life that this book is largely about.

When I began writing, I had a completely different book in mind. I tried to write that book, but ended up writing instead about what is interesting to me today—not what interested me two years ago when this book proposal was accepted. I found that there was more power in the current unknown depths where I'm exploring, instead of in the known shallows of last year and the years before those.

I was also surprised that I had to write so intimately, meaning from me to you. I had expected to write something with a much more obvious scientific grounding, and offer everything in authoritative phrases based on other people's research as a crutch to support my own.

And then one day early on in the writing process, the thought, *It's just like Bird by Bird,* popped into my head. While it's been years since I read Anne Lamott's book about the art of writing, what I distinctly remember is that it's her very personal account of what it *feels* like to write. She's less concerned with giving people a technical how-to, involving plots and grammar, than simply sharing her experience of what it means to have this creative art in her life. You don't learn to *write* from her; you learn to *become a writer*.

In Lamott's method, I saw the parallel to what I teach: the art of creative Flowdreaming, or manifesting. Over the years, I've laid out the fundamentals of Flowdreaming and Flowthinking in another book, eight CDs, and almost 250 hours of radio shows. Here, I won't be teaching you *how* to manifest; I'll be teaching you how to *become a manifester*. (For some of you, this may lead you to becoming a manifesting practitioner, too. Others may simply dabble in the art as needed.)

I have an intense interest in laying out a picture of what it's like to live and work within what I call the Flow—of which Flowdreaming is an important aspect. Like Lamott, I find myself sharing my thoughts and speculations with you. And almost every time I sit at my keyboard, musing over one nuance or another of this practice, I try not to feel afraid that revealing to you honestly and candidly what I *don't* know will usurp the credibility of what I *do* know. I want to share my own doubts as well as the shimmering breakthroughs that often came on the heels of those doubts.

The truth is that there's still so much to discover; in fact, we're still just learning how to ask the right questions. So I'll push you toward thinking about the things I'm thinking about. I'll relate stories and examples. I'll tell you about lines of thinking that have opened new doors for me and taken me beyond many of our traditional ways of understanding our world. And I'll let you know why I think these ideas may be true, as well as about cherished beliefs that no longer seem valid at all.

I was shocked several years ago when I realized that this idea of Flow, which so much in our lives centers on, has made me completely overthrow the majority of my past spiritual beliefs. It's as if the basis of my spirituality has been ripped apart so that a new understanding can take hold. I'm now going against the grain of most popular alternative religious practices and thought. What I've been led to believe clashes with the popular interpretations of reincarnation; ghosts; karma; evil; out-of-body and psychic experiences; and other Eastern, Western, and New Age beliefs. I didn't try to do this. It was the fallout from probing a very specific process—Flowdreaming.

Flowdreaming was the door that led to another universe.

There are many books today that use cutting-edge scientific research to discuss the idea that you can shape your reality with your mind. Everything is "quantum" this and "quantum" that. However, once it's been scientifically established and brought out into the mainstream that you *can* change things—manifest—through the power of your consciousness, then what? I hope to open your mind to the possibilities that lay ahead. I want you to consider things that are brand new and possibly shocking. I want you to learn how to work with and shape the energies we are all made from. I want you to have hope and even enthusiasm for what this means for your life.

At the very least, you're going to read the innermost musing of one woman's mind as she's undergone certain strange experiences and reached conclusions based on her observations. You will be introduced to new ideas, or at least new interpretations of very old ideas. Ultimately, you'll come away with an intimate portrait of how one person on this planet is living her life.

The book is organized in three parts. In the first, I've explained and defined such concepts as the Flow, Flowdreaming, and manifesting. The second part presents Flowdreaming in a larger context and shows where it's taken me through the years—the real-world effect I've experienced from living so intimately in the Flow. Part III, "Musings," is a collection of essays that gives examples of where Flow energy has been especially stimulating for me.

I've curbed the scientific jargon in *Creative Flowdreaming* because I want you to think from the gut. I wanted to write as if you and I were having dinner with friends. During this type of conversation, we'd feel comfortable exploring the boundaries of our beliefs; we'd be stimulated by thinking about our friends' views and how they differ from our own. We'd be open with each other because we'd feel safe—no one would be trying to convert us or make us defensive.

I hope you'll identify with some of what I've written here. I really do believe that everything I've seen and felt, others have seen and felt, too. I draw many parallels to the natural world, and it's possible that some natural scientists may not completely agree with arguments I've made . . . or they may find further overlooked similarities. My analogies are meant to point out tendencies and natural parallels, to show how systems reflect each other, and how all life is part of the same interconnected system. What I'm doing is trying to draw you in to look at life from a particular perspective that offers great power as opposed to struggle or victimization. How we live our lives is ultimately a choice. May the art of creative Flowdreaming become yours.

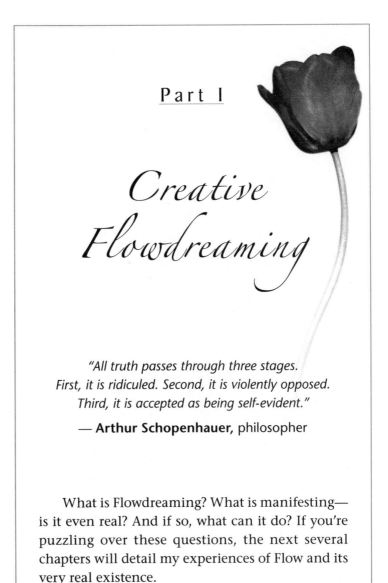

Part I

Creative Flowdreaming

"All truth passes through three stages.
First, it is ridiculed. Second, it is violently opposed.
Third, it is accepted as being self-evident."

— **Arthur Schopenhauer,** philosopher

What is Flowdreaming? What is manifesting—
is it even real? And if so, what can it do? If you're
puzzling over these questions, the next several
chapters will detail my experiences of Flow and its
very real existence.

Chapter 1

Who Are You?

You are in a constant state of creation and re-creation. You don't even realize it, but in every moment, your thoughts are impacting the environment around you, subtly shaping the paths that lay ahead.

Most likely, you were raised to believe that your thoughts were somehow trapped inside your head. You thought them, they were stored in memory, and that was it. Done.

Today, a new model of consciousness has emerged: our thoughts and emotions are tools used to sculpt a field of energy in, around, and through us. What we think isn't just contained in our brains, but our thoughts exist in an expanded mind field that permeates space at a quantum level and which interacts with this space every second.

The signals our mind broadcasts become our medium* for expression, much as an artist uses paint to transmit her art to the world. You communicate your "design" for life through your feelings and beliefs about yourself and your life.

By opening this book, you've shown that you're curious about this new way of thinking. You want practical tools to better sculpt this life of yours. And so as you explore the idea of manifesting, you'll discover that there does in fact exist a means for you to impact your life, beyond what you've always been told.

First, you'll learn about Flow—what it is and how to use it. You'll discover what it means to become a manifesting practitioner, and then use the energy of Flow to create new and positive life developments. You'll move from being a victim to being a powerful creator, able to affect the unfurling of your future as you attract what you desire.

After you pick up these ideas and begin to work with them, we'll dive into deeper waters as I introduce concepts to you that have arisen from the many years I've worked with the Flow. This is where we'll move from learning what manifesting is to *becoming a manifester.*

One concept you'll be introduced to is that we're allowed to construct our lives however we want. What a basic idea, right? And yet . . . so often we find ourselves "caught up" in other people's expectations and ideas. We find ourselves pushing against social limits and economic barriers. And worse, we limit ourselves, unknowingly, with our own expectations. We rarely treat ourselves as well as we treat others. We love others more than we love

---

Medium refers to a substance through which signals can travel as a means for communication, such as the different media artists use to create with: paint, pencil, ink, and so on—not to a psychic.

ourselves, and this too translates into the situations in our lives, reflecting how we are always complacent about taking "second best."

Another idea I'll discuss is that we don't have to live life as if it were a series of challenges, or go through "learning experiences" for "growth"—or even that we have to be miserable in order to advance our soul. Suffering is just one of many choices we have; it's not mandatory (although we certainly seem to just blunder into it a lot).

Like a Buddhist, you're going to come to see suffering as an emotional choice—a response you choose—to certain circumstances in your life. Most of these situations can easily be changed, and you'll realize your power over them. No longer a victim of seemingly random tragedies, you'll gain great confidence.

You'll also learn how to develop your life as a pattern of experiences, and program in the ones you desire so that they'll come to pass. Life won't be seen as a series of positive and negative events; instead, by working with this design, you'll discover how to choose certain conditions to explore or avoid. You'll be able to choose the people, home, work, health, and other situations you want to experience for a while. Then when you're satisfied that you've tasted all there is of that particular setup, you'll move on to a new pattern. Looking at life as a series of patterns of experience frees you up to accept the many kinds of situations that enter your life, without having to judge yourself over each one. For instance, when you lose your job, you don't have to feel that you've somehow "slipped down a rung" . . . nor is it a permanent condition. You're simply entering a new pattern of experience for a while, and you have the power to decide how long that state will last. Will you stick it out, eking out all the misery you can from it? Or will you focus intensely on leaving this pattern and entering a new one where you're appreciated, happy, fulfilled, and well paid?

Another way to look at life is that it's not vertical, or a linear ladder to be climbed—it's horizontal. You can cover a lot of ground as you navigate through life without an upward struggle. You're not trying to get somewhere or learn lessons to fix yourself; you're exactly where you should be right now, living what you've created in your life until this point. The people, objects, and things surrounding you are all here at your request, or at the very least, your permission.

Last, you'll discover a new way of looking at Source energy and how God, or Source, can move beyond the usual persona as a loving, benevolent force into something that offers you pure, raw, creative power. God becomes your paintbrush.

We cover a lot of ground because I want to show you what it really means to work with the energies of life. Since I wrote my first book, *Flowdreaming,* in 2003, there has been an explosion of books about manifesting; emotion; intention; and, in particular, the intersection of quantum theory with human potential. Ideas that I presented back then have become almost mainstream, and many prominent scientists have joined the discussion by writing their own fascinating interpretations of how our thoughts truly do affect the state of our universe. This concept no longer needs proof to gain acceptance—when even Oprah has begun talking about how our world is influenced by our thoughts, the next step has certainly come.

Now that we've begun to move past the "prove it to me" point, we can start to examine what it's like to fully incorporate these ideas into our lives. Why do some things happen when we wish them to, while others don't? Why do some of our dreams seem to manifest so quickly, when others seem like they'll never happen? How can we best do this thing called "manifesting"? Why do we suffer? Why can't we control or plan everything? How do other people's thoughts affect us? And what is life like from the perspective of the vast Flow of interrelated energies?

Let's begin exploring.

Chapter 2

What Is Manifesting, and What Is Flow?

Throughout this book, you'll notice that I don't often share the stories of others. That's because this journey has been my own voyage of discovery. Along the way, I've introduced the ideas I'm sharing with you to millions of people all around the world, mostly through my radio program, *Flowdreaming,** and my Website, **Flowdreaming.com.** But this has been merely a resultant benefit—the real story lies within myself. So in order to introduce you to the Flow, first I'll tell you how *I* was introduced to it.

The concept of manifesting has been in my life since birth. Of the particular set of opportunities I came into this world with, one was a family in which metaphysical

---

*The weekly hour-long radio program, *Flowdreaming,* can be heard on **HayHouseRadio.com®**.

ideas were the staple of dinner conversation. I also recall going to our Catholic church for weddings, funerals, and baptisms on my father's side of the family, as well as Baptist Sunday school after he remarried. My mother supplemented this education by having us spend time with various small spiritual denominations, many far removed from the mainstream. We were even involved with a cult for a while.

My childhood was rich with spiritual fodder. It was as if I was given a huge palette of beliefs to explore—from the mundane to the downright kooky. From a very early age, I was able to compare beliefs and search for the seed of "truth" in each one.

Later, I was attracted to nature religions that recognized the inherent force existing in all life. Some inner part of myself intuited that all things, living and so-called dead, were imbued with an energy of *being,* as yet unnamed. While these nature religions acknowledged this inner connection, I felt that the dogmas surrounding the practices were artificial and often self-serving. The power of the mind, however, and how it interacts with life and the energies around us, continued to possess me.

Years later, as more scientists began unraveling the stuff that life is made of, a new explanation began circulating that was anchored in quantum physics. Some scientists now asked, "What are we really made of?" "What is there that's deeper than the atom, the electron, or the quark?" "Where does it all begin?" and "Where does it end?"

Their answers have been stunning, even involving the nature of reality itself and how consciousness not only perceives it, but creates it.

MANIFESTING HAS HAD MANY SURGES OF POPULARITY over the years, from the relatively recent fads to the quiet messages found in older religions that have been practicing this since the beginning of civilization. As our own era progressed, new philosophers, metaphysicians, and authors reintroduced the idea and began to comment on the energy connection we make with our desires. The stage was set for the science that has since swept through and provided a basis for it all.

When I think about how the concept of Flow came to me, I can see it as a natural progression, much like the end point of a domino set of experiences coming to fruition. Over the years my actions, interests, and thoughts cut a channel, like a stream through mud, that led me to my current understanding of Flow. Like most people, I was "manifesting unaware" in my life—it just so happens that the end result of this particular manifesting led to *an awareness of the process itself.*

Long ago I learned how to practice the more popular means of manifesting: meditation, creative visualization, affirmations, spell casting, prayer, ritual, and so on. Each of these had promised a way to change or alter my reality based on my thinking or desire. I had tried most of these techniques, none of which I was completely satisfied with.

I found that when I prayed, I often became a supplicant, asking a power that I supposed was higher than myself to consider whether I was worthy enough to receive what I asked for. I felt essentially powerless.

I discovered that when I meditated, I'd get frustrated and angry at myself because my mind became unusually chatty. My mind is always yapping, like a dog barking for attention. And so I'd spend what little time I had to meditate battling my own thoughts and feelings as I grew more upset at my apparent lack of ability to meditate. It was like going against the grain of my mind's natural rhythm. Again, I would finish feeling powerless, this time over my own mind.

When I did "spells" or rituals for manifesting, I felt a little silly invoking deities I had no connection to. The whole process seemed steeped in the dogma of yesteryear, and it felt as if I were performing the nostalgic rehashing of pagan rituals reconstructed by some charismatic leader. It was fun, but ineffective. However, I did enjoy the aspect of anchoring desired energies into the physical world through ritual.

If I did affirmations, I'd have the feeling that while I had truly changed my subconscious thinking, I was still not seeing my desires translate into my experiences.

Even the practice of creative visualization always left me wondering if the imagery I was generating was actually doing anything or going anywhere. Unsure of how detailed I should be getting, I'd see what I wanted; focus on all the aspects of the scenario down to the colors, textures, locations, and people involved in what I was wishing for; and then open my eyes and think, *So did that actually do anything?* Because I didn't feel any different. However, occasionally I'd become so involved in the imagery that my heart would leap up and fill me with exuberance. I'd feel an intense inner connection to what I wanted, seeing it as already having come to pass. Only then would I feel that I was actually on to something.

When I first began to practice the art of manifestation, I tried all the aforementioned techniques. Eventually, I began to practice daily, with my mother as my support— much like a "diet buddy" whom you call every day just to make sure you don't succumb to cake and soda. She and I settled on a form of creative visualization that was tinged with our particular family's nuances.

One day as we were guiding each other through our visualization, we experienced something very different, almost as if we'd been "taken" somewhere. Soon after, I named this sensation "the Flow." Our encounter with the Flow opened the door to some spectacular spiritual revelations, and heralded such a shift that we even encountered otherworldly energies as we sought to understand it.

As I've already described in detail in my first book, *Flowdreaming*, my initial exploratory encounter with the Flow led me to begin working intensely with it. Soon, I realized that it was hugely impacted by emotion. From there, I discovered that I achieved my most potent manifesting through a combination of three powerful ingredients—a trinity of the Flow, daydreaming, and emotion—that when combined yielded the most potent manifestation tool I had ever experienced. I named this powerful combination "Flowdreaming."

The First Component of Flowdreaming: the Flow

The first of the three components was simply an awareness of the Flow. Flow is a name for a powerful energy that not only permeates all things but *is* all things; it refers to the deeper essence of everything around us. In a sense, the Flow, Source energy, and God are interchangeable. The Flow is a way of pinpointing or naming the unbound creative potential of that energy, much the same way we refer to the Holy Spirit as a facet of, but not separate from, God. The Flow *is* Source energy, but it is distinguished by characteristics that make it an ideal medium for carrying or materializing our desires.

You can think of the Flow almost as a substance that can be guided, like a sculptor molds clay. When I say that in Flowdreaming you create an energetic template, blueprint, or pattern—that you *program* this substance—I'm really saying that you'll be laying out a set of instructions that will tell your Flow how to behave next and what to create in your life. Your Flow, in return, will tell you what's easiest and best for you, as well as how to obtain your desires in the simplest way.

Now, it can seem like a radical idea to use the energy of God Itself, Source, to create with—that you have the power to direct or guide God energy. But if you think about it, you do this already. Everything in our universe is made of God energy because God did not create it with materials outside of Itself. So as you hold this book, you know the paper is brimming with God energy. This is the first profound idea that the Flow reveals to you: everything is made of Source energy, and you manipulate it every day.

It helps to think of the world—of our universe—as nothing but a swarming mass of quantum energy. Even those so-called empty places in space have recently been shown to contain vast amounts of energy. Everything we can see, man-made or not, is made of the same basic stuff no matter what eventual form it will take—this includes all things tangible and intangible. It's all just different accumulations and patterns of the Flow, or God, energy.

It's important to realize that this energy isn't static, unchanging, or frozen in place. Every one of these bits of organized energy (be it a frog, a cupcake, a quasar, you, or me) has a trajectory—a natural, organic direction in which it moves. This direction is distinguished by three obvious properties: ease, evolution, and increasing complexity. (There are many other properties inherent in the Flow, but these three create the basis for manifesting.)

Consider our universe: since inception, it's been growing, expanding, and evolving. Its trajectory is to blossom into galaxies with intelligent life, warmed by suns that eventually die as the galaxies are sucked into black holes that change and redistribute matter. But everywhere there is a *here* that will lead to *there*. We exist in a continuum of time where all events are given an opportunity to play out in their entirety along a path of ease and evolution. Time's arrow pushes us all along equally.

Our own world coalesced from gases consolidating to form a dense ball that evolved into land and atmosphere, eventually bringing life in ever-greater complexity. And while the planet has suffered setbacks and extinctions, it remains far more advanced and complex than the original stir of gases from whence it came.

When we look at our own ecosystems here on Earth, we see evolving complexity usually following the path of least resistance. Life *flows* down paths of evolution, just as water flows down to the sea. Seasons flow naturally from one to the next—nature enjoys balance and harmony despite the occasional upset (whether a cyclone or random cell mutation). Ease, expansion, and variety . . . this is the phase we're in. Perhaps someday this will reverse in the far distant future, and we'll all experience resistance, contraction, and reduction as the overriding wave of the universe, but that day is not here.

As part of this grand design, the ever-unfolding wave of God energy, we also follow our own paths, or Flows, forward. You can imagine this path as your personal energy signature. When you become aware of your Flow, you open yourself up to a smooth, peaceful path of harmony that's fundamental to your being. By aligning with your Flow, you simultaneously align with the great river of Source. You're but one tiny prick of conscious awareness within a much larger body: a small Flow within a much greater Flow. Think of your Flow like a small stream winding its way through a much larger ocean. Or think of a thick rope, made of many individual strands wound together. The rope is whole, the strands are separate. Humanity is the rope, and each individual is a strand within it. Or, enlarge your view: the universe is the rope, Earth is a strand within it. Or, larger still: God is the rope, and all things are strands within it. Your personal Flow is distinguished by your personal consciousness, but you occupy part of this larger, magnificent Flow, too. This means *you* are magnificent!

And like all things, as you move through life you're shooting forward in your Flow, traveling on a path of constant creation. In every second that ticks by, you're re-creating your life. Everything around you is likewise pulling itself into existence, second by second. Your Flow, like all Flow, also follows the path of ease, evolution, and increasing complexity. It will always seek the best path for you—the most natural and least energy-expending route to fulfill your Flow-aligned desires. This means that if you put your effort into something that is harmonious with your Flow, you'll be rewarded with obstacle-free experiences. Just as water never climbs uphill, you'll find yourself discovering that the most pleasurable and rewarding path to your goal is not an uphill slog.

In each moment, you're evolving into a state of greater complexity and adding to the sum total of yourself. Every thought you have is added to your consciousness. Think of a blanket being constantly knitted, stitches flying in every second. This is you, growing and expanding almost without effort—you don't even have to try. You just *are* this ever-growing consciousness; it's your nature.

So, your Flow embodies all this. Think of it as a line of energy moving forward, with the leading edge always fuzzy with the potential of "next." Sense your Flow behind you, like seeing the wake of a boat, as you build on and expand the energy signature of "you." Feel your presence in the Flow right now, and experience the surge of powerful forward motion toward tomorrow via a wave of ease, expansion, and fulfilled desires as you move into your future. The feeling of being in the Flow is one of perfect unity, protection, power, speed, agility, love, pleasure, creative expansiveness, and even ecstasy.

A Christian I know once expressed this idea beautifully to me. She said, "Being in my Flow is like lying down in God's river and allowing Him to take me wherever He wants." She puts all her trust in this river, which is essentially God's love. By doing so, she clearly expresses her desires and believes that God answers her through guiding her in her Flow (and His) toward the fulfillment of all her wishes.

The Flow, in its largest sense (whether you call it "Source energy," "God's love," "quantum energy," or any other label), is a fertile realm of pure creative possibility. For me it's like a *place,* since it's easier for my mind to comprehend it that way. Another way to envision it is to sense it like a net of energy coursing through the world or universe, rife with creative potential. Whenever we cast our thoughts or desires into this net, it responds by offering us back corresponding situations in the physical. So if you desire something, align yourself in your Flow's path of ease and clarity, then plant your desire within it. Then imagine that just like a seed in fertile ground, this desire seeks out all the "nutrients" or complementary conditions it needs to fruit into being, using the resources of the vast ocean of energy around it.

The Second Component of Flowdreaming: Guided Daydreaming

So how do you access this Flow, this "place"? I already hinted that your consciousness is the door in, but how do you take that first step?

The second component of Flowdreaming is something that I named *guided daydreaming*. When we daydream, we allow our minds to enter a place of unbridled potentiality. It's the closest we come to childlike creation, where we forget to place limits on outcomes. We let ourselves go, without inhibition or prohibition, as daydreaming takes us to an altered state.

When you daydream, your brain waves often move into the same altered state as during light meditation. When you daydream with conscious direction, however, you can move into the same state of heightened awareness and efficiency that inspires athletes to peak performance or scientists to their "Eureka!" moments.

Just as those in deep meditation have a subjective experience far beyond what is scientifically measurable, the same is true when daydreaming in the Flow—the experience transcends explanation.

Highly focused, directed daydreaming opens a pathway in your thinking by creating a conduit to emotional, focused consciousness that becomes your palette for creating or shaping deeper energies.

Entering the Flow

The process for reaching your Flow through guided daydreaming is deceptively simple. First, close your eyes and allow your mind to drift, just as you would when entering a daydream. Bring up imagery that conveys the feeling of your Flow to you.

In my case, I see and sense a rolling river of light moving purposefully forward. I recognize this as the fundamental energy of myself and my life as it unfurls ahead of me, and I feel myself being carried along, peacefully and effortlessly. It's as if I reach that place where my life is in its ideal form, where everything always works out for my best and greatest fulfillment. I feel completely in tune with my Greater Self or what you may call Source or God's will.

I see this powerful field of energy that surges and moves along as *my life in progress,* as it unfolds moment by moment. I don't sit and wait for something magical to "show up" when I close my eyes—*I create it.* I *go* there by constructing my own imagery and sensation for it.

By doing this, I "open a door" to another realm, but it's up to me to input my own imagery in this realm, which is beyond our three-dimensional world. My mind has to translate this unfathomable place, this deep energy state, into imagery that it can understand. It's like staring at a color you've never seen before. You can't even imagine this new hue accurately, so you'd probably end up "fitting" it into something your mind could deal with by translating it into a known color your eyes could actually see. Such is the case with the Flow. *You must create your own little scenario of what your Flow looks and feels like to you.* You daydream it, and this daydream becomes the interface between you and it.

BEFORE CONTINUING ON, I want to answer two common questions: "What does the Flow look like?" and "How do I know if I'm really there?"

As I already noted, your mind creates beautiful pictures to describe what is fundamentally nonphysical to help you process the information. Your brain is simply not made to grasp these deep inner states of reality. Your brain is an antennae, trying to read the scramble of information through the bridging mechanism of your mind. You'll see images that carry meaning, but the visuals themselves are fundamentally unimportant. It's what they make you *feel* that's important. This is why I tell you to make up the imagery of your Flow. Make it up at first, then as you "arrive" there, it will very likely—but not always—take on a life of its own.

When I "see" my Flow, it often morphs into many different representations of itself. I have been doing this for so long that I often become immediately caught in the *feeling* of being carried within a powerful river of energy, without even seeing it. If I do stop to look, I see a moving current of sparkling light pushing powerfully forward. Surrounding this are what appear to be strings of light, weaving in and out in patterns of sparkling intensity. To me this represents the powerful, ongoing nature of reality as it creates itself, while the strings show me how energy is merging and disengaging as new conditions and situations continually emerge.

However, this is just *my* way of sensing the energy in motion. Other people have told me that they see themselves upon a walkway or shining path that leads them purposefully forward. Some have said that they're floating in deep space, pulled forward by an invisible force, while others have told me that they're in fields of flowers. One woman who lives in Alaska even told me she was on a river with friendly brown bears all around her.

The Flow is a place of two-way communication, so you may discover imagery and sensations that seem to carry a message for you. When you access the Flow for purposes of manifesting, you're often so busy *sending* data into it that you don't pause to listen for the data you're meant to *receive*. But it does, and will, come to you. Depending on what this information is, you'll ask questions like, "What does a waterfall mean?" "What does a whirlpool mean?" "Why am I not moving?" or "Am I going too fast?" These images or sensations are messages as to how the energies in your life are flowing. Things such as waterfalls or whirlpools may mean that some aspect of your life feels out of control. Or perhaps you've involved yourself in something that's "sucking you in."

The key is to ask yourself, *What feeling accompanied that image? Was I scared? Upset? Angry? Feeling rushed?* If your Flow is moving you at a slow pace, and your life is likewise not going anywhere, then you can see the clear energy connection between the Flow sensation and reality.

On the opposite end, if you're being whipped along, avoiding rushing debris, hitting rapids, upset or scared, then the message is that this is the current state you're in. Recognizing this allows your Flow to return to its original, divine pace. *You* are the one rushing or spinning or falling, not your Flow; it's just showing you what you're doing. Change the vision and see yourself gliding forward softly on skis or floating in a lounge chair. It makes no difference what "stage decor" you use.

One important sensory aspect you want to try to experience is of a pleasant, powerful, forward-feeling sensation or lift. The feeling of moving ahead along a line of existence helps you recognize that you, like everything else, are in fact going through time and space along a trajectory. This course is your particular Flow, your defining energy state, and there is perfection in this. If you have trouble getting this feeling of progress going, allow your body to sway slightly forward and back as you envision your Flow. Or summon the feeling of being on a roller coaster—the way your body is moved forward, aligned on a track.

You'll know that you've reached your Flow when you feel this alignment occurring. Sometimes the sensation is visceral, like being swept up and carried away. Other times the sensation is of release, a powerful "unlocking" that lets go of you. Many times you'll feel your Flow as a *presence* around you. It's different for each of us, and is one of those know-it-when-you-see-it experiences.

Don't get frustrated if you only dip in and out of your Flow for a while. You'll bring up the imagery, daydream, and try to feel it; but it will be like bouncing on a trampoline, trying to touch the ceiling with your hand. You'll hit it occasionally, but afterward will be left wondering *Was I really there?* To this question I'd say worry less about the validity of your experience and focus instead on the next important aspect: cultivating your emotions.

The Third Component of Flowdreaming: Emotion

Once you've allowed the imagery of your Flow to develop in your guided daydream, put your awareness into *feeling* your Flow. Positive emotion is the third key aspect of the trinity that defines the technique of Flowdreaming. (Again, the three components of Flowdreaming are an awareness of Flow, guided daydreaming, and strong emotion.)

The *feeling* you encounter in your Flow is even more important than any imagery. Feeling is what attaches you to, and puts you *in,* this place. Daydreaming is the interface that opens the door; emotion keeps you creating within it.

In the Flow, you can let your emotional antennae feel ahead to sense the potential in your life—all the people, situations, and events that may happen as you travel toward them in your great river of energy. It's like looking into the face of creation: you'll feel the movement and change of every second of life; the potential ahead; and the sensations of being carried forward, buoyed up, protected, guided, and supported. It's an excited feeling of anticipation for the future and recognition of the present all at once.

And as you feel your future unrolling before you, you'll realize that it doesn't have to be cloudy or unknown. It can contain whatever information you choose to put there. You can request or program whatever experience you'd like to encounter—whether it's one second or 20 years away. Realize that in this place, creation is actively being put into place, whether you're aware of it or not. Now, being aware, you can choose to add your personal requests. This is the heart of manifesting.

The Coding In of Emotion

I create my personal requests through the coding in, or programming, of *emotion.* Think of emotion as a language like computer code. Emotion, like code, both gives and receives instructions to and from the operating system of the Flow. Emotion very effectively communicates a huge amount of information instantaneously, bypassing the hindering use of language. It communicates *directly to Source.*

For instance, when you try to describe the feeling of love, you often find yourself at a loss for words. You could talk for days trying to describe its every nuance, but this will never yield you the actual experience that transcends language. As a tool that carves and shapes energies, strong, directed emotion exceeds not only words, but images and thoughts as well.

Our culture has conditioned us to mistrust our emotions and suppress them. Women are still told that we need to "get control of ourselves." We've been instructed not to be manipulative with our feelings, and warned that being emotional is an underhanded power grab designed to make others feel guilty. We've been punished for being "too emotional." We've been told to just stuff our feelings and be nice.

Men, too, have been taught that feeling deep emotions is unmanly; it's wimpy and girly. They're required to be tough and keep their emotions in check. Men don't cry.

These cultural directives have made our emotional selves into our adversaries. Rather than being a source of immense power, our emotions are devalued and repressed.

As a mom, I know that helping my young children learn to control their own emotions is a key part of my parenting. It must be done. The difference is that I can teach them to use and listen to their emotions instead of simply shutting them down (or feeling bad or guilty for having them).

Branching out, society itself has had good reason to corral us into repressing our emotions. People are more easily controlled when they don't have strong feelings to express. It's easier for groups to get along, not go to war, and otherwise "play nice"—especially when there are powerful groups with a vested interest in controlling human behavior: politicians, dictators, religious leaders, and corporations, to name a few.

However, all this cultural emphasis on emotional control has come at a cost. It's robbed us of the power to use our emotions as a creative tool. We've never been taught *how* to use these tools. In your Flow, you use your emotions like a carpenter uses a hammer or a saw.

Imagine each emotion in your toolbox as having a particular function. For example, the feeling (tool) of *deserving* creates an openness in your future to receiving, like opening the windows to let the sun shine into your home. Likewise, the feeling (tool) of *thankfulness* acknowledges that you've already received that which you desire. Thankfulness carves in an energy of, "It's a done deal."

On the other hand, the feeling (tool) of *want* creates a feeling of desire. Desiring is not the same as receiving, so when you pour deep desire—longing—into your Flow, then your Flow will seek to create all the situations it can find to continue giving you more longing.

Instead, you can use the emotions of *claiming* and *ownership,* which include feelings of satisfaction, pride, thankfulness, joy, and a sense of "looking back" as if something has already come to pass. Then your Flow will seek to line up situations that reflect all of those feelings. (Incidentally, for many people this basic confusion of generating longing—*wanting* versus *having*—is the single biggest factor in their inability to manifest.)

Programming the energies with your emotion means that you're preselecting the emotional states that you want to play out for you as you move through life. I'll tell you more about using your emotions as tools as we move ahead. For now, take a look at the chart at the chart called

Emotional States and Their Uses in the back of the book, which shows some of the most effective emotions you can experience in the Flow.

Putting It Together

As I said, the process of Flowdreaming is incredibly simple. No aspect is difficult. I use this process of guided, conscious daydreaming to allow my mind to interface with these deeper, more fundamental energies of life called the Flow. I simply call to mind the feeling of this place, then allow my daydreaming mind to populate it with whatever visuals make it engaging and interesting. Finally, I begin feeling the experience of placing my desires into it using the tool of emotion.

The trinity of the Flow, daydreaming, and emotion is the basis of Flowdreaming. You know what emotion feels like (although the idea of using emotions may be new), you know how to daydream (although you never lose yourself in the daydream the way you normally would—it's more like lucid dreaming), and now you know about Flow. The next questions are, "How do we know the best content to program?" and "How do we know what to ask for?" To answer that, you need to learn how to design your life from a Flow perspective.

Chapter 3

Designing a Life

It seems to me that there are really only two kinds of living. One is the haphazard, come-what-may way in which you tumble from one thing to the next, randomly adding and changing bits of your life with only cursory thought. We spend most of our time reacting to events "outside our control" and ducking or avoiding everything else. Sometimes we'll ask for things willy-nilly, one after another, like buying mismatching shirts and pants because it strikes us that we like that thing in front of us, even if it doesn't "go" with anything else we own. Our life is a random mess of avoidance, desire, and fulfillment, and a lot of just plain reactive living.

In the other kind of living, each experience is sought out or at least weighed for value. This life is *designed*. It's the difference between walking into a messy, chaotic living room and one that has had a professional makeover. The made-over room is purposeful; it has a character to convey.

My life has been a mix of both, as I think most people's have been. Some years I took what I bumped into, while others showed signs of true cultivation.

As I sat in the sun this morning watching my son play in the yard, I thought about my life's current design. I realized that all the major pieces are almost in play, although I need to pull a few "weeds" (eliminate a few minor situations that aren't working for me) and can see that some "plants" (situations or things that occupy too much of my time) need some serious pruning back. Now it's a matter of bringing in a final few missing elements, and then farther down the road I see the possibility of turning in a new direction, but where that is I've yet to decide. This is me looking at my life from a larger viewpoint.

Much like you tend to the elements of your retirement by overseeing your assets and investments, you manage the design of your life through careful monitoring and assessment. It's not a chore; it's a delight. The idea that you can cultivate a life that pleases you should be so ingrained within you that even as you read this, you should be saying, "Of course I already know that." Yet for so many people, the journey has been like a dinghy ride through high waves as they constantly just barely make it.

Design often requires negotiation with yourself. Just as a pretty room has an element of control to it (the colors are harmonious and the furniture is of the same style), sometimes you'll need to put back on the shelf certain desires that fundamentally wreck the character of the room. Seek a natural congruency, a harmony when hanging together the elements in your life. For example, you probably won't be able to have both a husband and a boyfriend. There's too much discord in that design, so you'll have to choose one or the other.

You also probably won't be able to own a gorgeous home overlooking the sea on a waitress's income. These two are not in alignment. You'll need to select a different home or manifest a job, mate, or other new situation that easily supports such a home.

Our desires are often in conflict with each other and we don't recognize it. We just know that *something isn't working*. So we must carefully observe our desires, and recognize the overall design we're going for, and be willing to see and search for these conflicts.

Everyone, without exception, has the ability to manifest the things they wish to experience. Life will continue to throw in lots of unexpected surprises—that is part of the game, too—but those surprises can be factored in to your overall picture. If you've generally designed a life of surplus and joy, then a year or two of unexpected privation will be much easier to bear.

We naïvely think that the choices we make day by day result in the life we see around us. In reality, the choices we make come at the end point of the game. In our daily lives, we simply select from the final set of opportunities before us—the array of choices that have already been defined for us to pick from. It's like a child choosing his morning outfit from the clothes his mother has already bought him versus going to a mall and choosing from the many more options; someone had to do the "winnowing down" for us. This happens in the gap between the idealism of our Flow and the decisions we make in the physical that regulate the possibilities we can experience. When you go to a deeper level and work directly in the Flow, you are vastly expanding your arena of choices. You're reaching out and programming the energies *before* they manifest into your limited set of options in the physical.

Honing In on the Design

Once you've thought about the relative design (or lack of design) in your life, your next step is to begin creating a "wish list" of desires. You've probably created this list already, but now that you're thinking in terms of the Flow and design, you may already be making changes. Maybe you're assuming that next I'm going to ask you to go through this list of objects and situations you're desiring and begin calling them into being in your Flow, or that I'll ask you to make a dream board with pictures of what you want in life or do some other popular self-improvement exercise. . . . Nope! Not so fast.

There's nothing inherently wrong with dream boards,* but there's also nothing more stifling for your Flow than to be given a mundane wish list of objects.

When you say you want a house on an ocean bluff and it must have white walls, brown trim, four bedrooms, and a handsome man (or gorgeous women) to meet you at the doorstep, you're narrowing down your field of potential. Every restrictive measure you offer your Flow reduces the field of possibility it has for you.

---

*A dream board or dream book is made from cutting out magazine photos or words and gluing them into a collage that represents your ideal life, whether career-wise, romantically, or lifestyle related. The idea is to periodically look at the board and concentrate on these images as a way to focus your intention on what you wish to manifest.

Instead, you must hone in on the most important qualities, situations, or objects you want to have in your life and
let go of the details. Focus purely on the emotions that you
think these things will generate in you, not the details of
the things themselves.

For example, what if you're single and think that there
are no good men or women left? You haven't dated in years
and are lonely, but you've basically given up. Finally you
decide that a romantic, generous, passionate, trustworthy,
communicative, sexy partner would be kind of nice to have
around. If you were writing a personal ad, you might think
about weight, height, hair color, proximity, marital status,
intelligence, education, profession, children, and so on as
requirements to jot down.

But what if instead, you're simply honed in on the
feeling that this person is a true match for you, the relationship is easy and passionate, you're always happy and
confident and trusting with this person, and you're genu-
inely head over heels with a great person who fulfills you
in every way? If this person you manifest through this
basic set of emotional requirements were to show up, then
by default they would be single (they would have to be, or
they wouldn't make you feel confident and trusting) and
they would be your physical "type" (they would have to be,
or you wouldn't feel such hot smoldering passion for them),
and so forth.

*The end goal is to focus on the emotional experience of
what you want, not the details of the literal physical thing or
situation.*

If you want to work from home so you have more time
to raise your kids but still be able to pay off your debt,
for instance, you wouldn't focus on the perfect envelope-
stuffing job coming to you. Instead, you'd see yourself

holding and hugging your kids at home and feeling your-self having lots of freedom as lots of money continually pours in from good sources. You'd feel how easy it is for you to do the work that brings you such a good income and how secure and stable it is. Most of all, you'd visualize you and your kids grinning with happiness at how nicely and smoothly your work/family balance has come about.

You may experience a sensory aspect, too, such as hug-ging your children, the smell of their hair, the scent of new $20 bills in your hand, or the sound of the phone ringing with joyful employers or clients on the line. These sensa-tions are also very powerful, so you should cultivate them whenever you can.

Another example is that you have a small struggling business and desperately need clients. For too long you've been allowing this feeling of desperation to exist in your Flow, creating dire situations. Instead, see yourself throw-ing your arms open to welcome the legions of happy clients and customers coming your way as more and more people are extolling your virtues and want your services, talking you up to all their friends and business associates. Happy people who *love* your products or services are flocking to you! They think that what you provide is worth every penny and happily pay you, pushing their money toward you. In return, you're so delighted that at the end of each day you see yourself sighing contentedly at how well the design has come together. Life is perfect.

Do you see how you're focusing on the end result—the *feeling* you have in each of these scenarios? Your Flow can arrange situations out of millions of possibilities, selecting the very best combinations of events for you. You don't even need to focus on *exactly what* kind of work you want, *exactly what* hours you'll work, *exactly what* health benefits you'll get, or *exactly how much* debt will get paid off and at what pace. All of that, by default, will be taken care of in the new design your Flow will work out for you. Your goal, defined in your Flow, is of a complementary work/home life (a feeling of balance), wealth (a feeling of security), plenty of time to be an unstressed parent (feelings of happiness/ fulfillment), and the ability to pay down all the bills (feelings of pride/relief). Each of these desires has an emotion that it triggers when you think of it.

Now what if you really want to focus on something *specific,* such as having a baby? That's fine, but just don't dwell on the details. Feel a healthy baby *moving* (sensory) inside you or your wife, the overwhelming *joy* (emotion) at finding out about the pregnancy, and the *relief* (emotion) at knowing how *healthy* (emotion) and *easy* (emotion) the whole pregnancy will be. Don't focus on the exact month the baby will be born, or its gender. Instead, feel the *excitement* (emotion) the baby is bringing you, what the word *invitation* (emotion) means as you welcome this little soul in, and yourself *holding* (sensory) this infant as you exude maternal or paternal feelings.

And then, if you encounter surprises during your progression toward this goal, you can make choices and focus your emotion on each decision as it arrives, such as: *I feel in vitro working out great! The best doctor is helping us. We are so lucky. I'm so happy I could laugh at how easily this was all solved.*

You can narrow your focus as you continue to make choices toward your goal. For instance, if you've seen yourself in the perfect home, fully delighted to walk into this place every day, and you finally find it and make an offer, then move on to the next step: *How easily this purchase transpires! How swiftly everything comes together. Everyone works together as a team; I'm so happy!*

So what's going on in each example? As you sketch out the designs in your life, you lay out the feelings you want to encounter within each area. You're focusing on the feeling—the end result—you want to see generated in any situation or area in your life. Allow your *Flow* to determine the best combination of events to bring those feelings into your life. Your job is to start with the final-result feeling and narrow it down into more specific episodes of happiness as you progress toward your goal. Another word for this process is *pre-action.*

The Power of Pre-action

All through our lives we're taught to react, and the faster and more intelligent the response, the better. In the evolution of humans and animals, a swift response was mandatory for survival. We reacted to predators by fighting or fleeing and to amorous advances by having intimate relations, thereby continuing the species. We react using our emotions, which guide us like a compass needle toward the most appropriate response much of the time . . . but not *all* the time.

Often, our emotional reactions are way out of balance with the trigger event or are completely inappropriate—usually because we learned an unhealthy habit of response from our families, such as the girl who learns to appease her alcoholic parent through a series of actions designed for short-term protection, but which result in long-term emotional scars.

Our habits of emotional reaction can help or hurt us, and we often have little awareness of exactly which of the two scenarios will play out as a result of our feelings. What's more, people expect us to react in socially approved ways. You can't laugh when you see someone get hurt (how rude or psychopathic!); you can't cry with misery when you're being congratulated. These responses are so outside the boundaries of what society expects that they'd be shocking. Our reactions have been heavily conditioned within us.

So what does this have to do with manifesting? I've thought about the power of emotions and our reactive natures for many years. Clearly, reaction has become our overwhelmingly dominant interaction with not just our environment and other people, but in every area, including the energetic underpinning of our lives. *Re*action means "responsive action," that we respond to something that's already occurred. If we live in a 99 percent reactive mode, then 99 percent of our energy is constantly engaged in dealing with the played-out scenario and not in programming the scenarios to come.

To design your life utilizing the deepest energies of the universe, a true manifesting practitioner must spend time on the other side of the coin: in *pre*-action. Pre-action is the counterpoint to reaction and the programming point, or place of initial ignition for the events and scenarios you will then *re*act to when they're expressed in the physical.

Pre-action is the emotional "pre-sponse" you have to the condition you're desiring and creating. In pre-action, you respond to the events or scenarios *before* they happen, not after. You program in the guidelines for the expression of what you want through your directed, focused, emotional pre-action. You feel the emotions of the end result of what you're desiring, set this energy condition into being, and then allow the physical expression of it to catch up; in essence, you're putting the cart before the horse. When you're in your Flow, your pre-action is what programs the energies and is the language of manifestation.

Let's go back to the example that you've been single and alone for a long time. You yearn for that partner you can explore life with, but you continually exude disappointment and negativity because your past experience of being alone has conditioned the *reaction* of these feelings in you. As you go forward each day, responses of disappointment, discouragement, fatalism, and unfulfilled longing radiate from you.

One day you decide that you'll experience a pre-action instead and emotionally program the energy around you to correspond with this intent. Even though a new person has yet to enter your life, you go straight the to finish line: you feel yourself happily in love with a partner who adores you. This person thinks you're incredibly smart, funny, good-looking, and compatible with him/her in every way, while you also feel everything you've been hoping for about a romantic partner.

Not only are you in love, but this is the easiest, most perfect, stable, and honest relationship you've ever been in and these feelings are now washing over you. Even though there isn't a face, location, or even a time line for this desire, you've gone straight to the result of the desire with these perfect feelings. You're pre-experiencing the thing you wish to manifest, and the emotions you express are a beacon that goes forth and begins creating the corresponding physical situation.

This idea of pre-action is fundamental to designing a life that continually blooms with the fruit of your completed desires. It's like you get to experience every emotion twice: first when you feel it in your pre-action, and then when you encounter the physical manifestation of it. Both sides of the encounter have been worked: the energy condition has been established and the physical condition has developed to match.

We are so used to working this equation backward. Every day in a thousand ways, we establish physical conditions first and then react energetically or emotionally to them. When we accidentally stub a toe, we react with pain and irritation; if we're having a conversation and say something we wish we hadn't, we react with self-doubt and self-condemnation. When we catch a glimpse of the billowing, sun-streaked clouds in the sky and the beauty of it overwhelms us, we feel a split second of awe. Reaction, reaction, reaction, both to so-called negative and positive experiences.

Life always shows us its duality: night and day, love and hate, black and white. It is only out of habit that we spend the majority of our time performing reactions instead of Flowdreaming pre-actions. We haven't developed the cultural heritage for pre-acting and creating—to learn this, we must create a new family tradition, in your life and in your children's lives, today. Now. You are full of power, you are full of creation, and you can program anything you want.

Chapter 4

Starting Your Manifesting Program

Now that you have a deeper understanding of the tools used for manifesting—such as the power of pre-action—and the associated emotions in your toolbox, let's return to the idea of the Flow state again.

It's up to each of us to discover our own perfect method for manifesting. Certainly, Flowdreaming is my preferred method since I've seen it accomplish so much in my life and the lives of others, but it also gives me an immediate, tangible feeling of having created. I know without a doubt that when I power my desires with an abundance of deep, strong, confident emotion within my Flow, that desire/emotion has now actually energetically affected the fabric of reality. The desire persists, has been added to the collective energy state, and continues on like a string of computer code that begins to replicate. I'm completely confident that when I put forth feeling in this specialized way, I'm creating something *real*. Each time I do this, I'm adding to the power of this desire, like a sand castle that grows each time more sand is put on it. Similarly, every time I have an emotionally fearful thought that's the opposite of what I want to create, it's like scooping the sand away and shrinking my castle.

A problem for many people who manifest is that once they're finished "wishing" for what they want, they forget about it for days or even weeks. Or they never acknowledge that what they're creating has a *realness* to it. It's as if they see their desires as being stuck in their own minds, small and ineffective, zipping around but going nowhere.

It helps to imagine that when you Flowdream, it's like you're sending out waves of colored ink. Imagine this ink seeping away from you, powerfully tinting the "air" around you. Now imagine that this ink is also tinting not just the air, but the very atomic structures within you and within our world. The ink has gone out and settled itself into various situations or objects or people that will become part of your future experience, as this ink is somehow coded to draw together all the parts it has sunk itself into. And each time you practice manifesting your desire, you add to the intensity of this ink. Now this isn't quite an accurate description of manifesting, but it can help you fundamentally *feel* how what you think carries a reality to it.

When you send out emotional instructions in your Flow, you're actively creating on a deeper level. It just so happens that when you finish, you can't see or hold what you just made, as you could if you drew a picture. But, like having a conversation, because you don't see it after it's over doesn't mean it didn't make an impact on your life, or won't go on having an effect.

Even your regular, everyday thoughts and emotions aren't safe in your own head. Thoughts exist in an expanded place where yours are as easily grabbed and read as a sheet of newspaper flying past in the wind. Fortunately, most people are not aware of this or we'd be living in a world of devoted mind readers; nonetheless, people's thoughts and intentions are there if you wish to access them.

How often have you felt things that you knew to be true, such as, "This person means me harm," or "This woman is hot for me"? Sure, people's bodies do send out nonverbal signals and hormones, but the bulk of the information we receive from each other is through our energy fields, and our energy field exists within our Flow. You know from past experience that when a person is romantically interested in you, you can somehow feel it. The information of attraction is carried in their scent, the dilation of their pupils, their body language, and possibly their words and gestures if they're consciously expressing it to you. But it's also carried in a more fundamental level of energy, and it's this level that accounts for the powerful "tug" you feel as a result of their interest. You can feel attraction for someone but then not see him or her for months or years, and when you encounter one another again, it's as if there's a snapping rubber band that jolts these old feelings back into you.

I often tell people that whatever thoughts they're carrying about themselves and others are written in neon on a marquee board they're invisibly holding up in front of their chest. When someone walks into a room to interview for a job, if he's thinking, *They aren't going to hire me because I really don't even want to work here . . . I have to get a job, so I guess this is as good as anything else,* then that's the first thing transmitted to the hiring director before he even shakes that person's hand. Forget nonverbal cues—what is your *Flow* telling someone? I remember counseling a woman once who'd been on 17 consecutive interviews without a job offer. "When you walk in the room and meet the hiring director," I asked her, "what are you thinking?"

"I'm thinking, *I hope you hire me but I bet you won't since the last 17 didn't.*"

"You might as well have just said it aloud and walked out of the room," I told her. "You immediately gave those people reason to doubt you before you even opened your mouth."

How real is this? How true is this? Well, consider for a moment how often you think a thought—it flits past your mind—and someone around you immediately comments on that very thought. Many people call it "coincidence," but I prefer to understand it within the context of the Flow. That is, your thoughts radiate around you.

Your psychic "filters" continually work to discard all the irrelevant nonverbal information buzzing around you, but everything that you're thinking or feeling exudes from you just as your body emits sweat and chemicals. Occasionally, a piece of information passes to you that vaguely catches your attention, like when the phone rings and before you pick it up, you say, "It's my sister." How did you know? Or when you wonder, *Why hasn't my husband called yet?* and the phone rings 30 seconds later—who was contacting whom?

I've had fun on occasion by "suggesting" certain ideas into people's minds. I simply spread strong, powerful intentional feelings while bringing a person to mind. I might picture them saying, "Summer deserves a real treat. I should really do something good for her; she needs it. I've noticed that she's feeling down lately and needs to feel valued and appreciated."

Doing this is like sending an invisible, energetic post-card to the person I'm thinking about, causing them to suddenly think, *Hmm. Summer seems like she could use a lift. I have an idea that would help her.* Or the next time I see them, the "postcard" of thought I sent them may trigger a response.

Time is irrelevant to when the "information packet" is opened, read, or activated; distance is also irrelevant. And it's not like we need to be psychic: we all send and receive such data *every moment of every day* as part of one layer of interaction we have with our world—the difference for me is that I'm aware of what I'm doing.

So when does this cross the line? What if I'm imagining harm and feeling angry at someone because he or she really upset me?

When I feel something, I surround myself with whatever energy I'm creating. I'm the generator, and what I generate spreads through my energy self and Flow to the same or even greater degree as it reaches whomever is the target of my anger.

The last time you became angry or upset, did you notice how stressed you became? How your stomach got upset, your mind blanked out, you developed a headache or got really exhausted, or you wanted a beer or cigarette or food? Any one of your unhealthy coping mechanisms may have gotten activated as you tried to bring down or alter the stress that the anger brought you. You become the container for any feelings you bring up, like a bottle filling with soda. You're surrounded by your own emotion.

A smart person is naturally cautious about how much negativity they want to create. In fact, an awareness of manifesting actually inhibits a true practitioner from doing any kind of negative Flowdreaming, since we know we're equally affected by it. It cannot be otherwise; we are what we think and feel.

So when I manifest, I bring to bear this understanding of the powerful, actual existence of my thoughts.

The Two-Week Program

Now that you have a grasp of the basics, how do you begin to practice Flowdreaming? Remember, it's an art: creative manifesting is the art of designing a life, and your medium is the fundamental energy of life itself. It can be daunting . . . which is why we start slowly with a set practice schedule and a two-week commitment.

It used to be that when people became interested in the Flow, I'd teach them the basics and tell them to just enter the state whenever it felt right, but I discovered that many people aren't comfortable with this. We are used to schools and classes, and programs of study where we're disciplined to attend at regular times. Without a structure to follow, it can make us feel insecure and unsure how to move forward, rather than liberated. So that's where the magic of the two-week challenge appeared.

I've successfully used this technique to help people manifest romance, money, wellness, and countless other good things into their lives. Basically, it goes like this: every day for two weeks you enter the Flowdreaming state for a minimum of ten minutes either once or twice daily. However, since this isn't meditation and you have to keep your mind focused and active within your daydream—while creating lots of strong, surging emotion—ten minutes can feel like forever.

At first, you may also struggle to stay within your daydream. Many new practitioners find themselves dipping in and out, there and gone, like a child falling off a balance beam, then getting back on, then falling off again. Your mind is used to daydreaming and drifting away. It's less used to drifting off on a choke chain of conscious awareness, so the experience of getting in the Flow in the beginning runs the gamut from absurdly easy for some people, to a frustratingly uneven experience for others.

However, unlike meditation, in which many people end up fighting their minds for "dominance" as their thoughts continue to stray, in Flowdreaming, most people are able to get into their Flow and at least get a good, ripe *feel* of it before they become distracted and drop out of the state. Keep in mind that there is no fighting for dominance over stray thoughts because you just enter the state again and again until the transition there becomes smooth and uninterrupted. If thoughts come up that do upset you (such as old worries or anxiety over something), you simply see them flowing away behind you, swirling out of your life. There is never any struggle or condemnation in your Flow. Ever. And at some point, you'll drift into your Flow deeply, and remain there comfortably in a charged, emotional state—and it won't take months or years of practice.

EACH DAY, CHOOSE A TIME when you're most likely to be undisturbed. Many people move into their Flow while out running or walking, or even as they work on a mindless task. These are excellent times to Flowdream since your mind is already primed to daydream or wander while your physical body is engaged in a repetitive experience.

I find that my best Flowdreaming occurs when I'm showering. As a mom, I have little time to myself, and my shower is the only point in the day when I have no demands on me. The falling water also helps facilitate the sensation of the Flow that I experience.

People often ask me if they can Flowdream before bed. My personal experience is that this isn't an especially fruitful time for it because your body is primed for sleep once it's in bed. It's used to reading, watching TV, praying, meditating, or any other "unwinding" and relaxing activity you normally do before going to sleep. Flowdreaming requires focus and effort—it isn't especially relaxing, although it can be for some people. It's helpful to calm your body before starting the process, but only so you won't carry any physical tension into your thinking.

Also, if you're in bed Flowdreaming or listening to my guided Flowdreaming CDs, you can easily fall asleep. Now, if you're listening to anything while sleeping, you're surely impacting your subconscious mind with powerfully suggestive material, but you're not engaging consciously in the Flow. You're "receiving" data, but Flowdreaming is a concentrated "sending" of data, and you're not doing that when your conscious mind is asleep.

Once you've chosen a time and place (such as while taking your morning walk during your break at work); committed to ten minutes daily for two weeks; recalled the three aspects of Flowdreaming (awareness of Flow, guided daydreaming, and strong emotional pre-action) you're ready to bring all three together for some powerful manifesting. So what are you Flowdreaming *for?*

When you begin to design your life, you won't want to tackle every area of your life at once. Choose one or two areas to fix first, which are usually areas that just aren't working in your life, since any area that isn't bringing you happiness is by default not in your Flow. (We'll go into that idea more later.)

Now, begin your two weeks of Flowdreaming. Expect to see things change . . . but not necessarily where you *think* they should change first. When you manifest in your life, you'll soon see that focusing on one area affects surrounding areas of your life, like dominoes falling. For instance, if you Flowdream to resolve a problematic situation with your lover, don't be surprised if another area of your life (such as your work) is impacted first. Think of a Rubik's Cube: to get all the squares on one side to match in color, you have to focus on how to turn the other sides so that the intended side will be impacted. A master of the puzzle will know to turn the cube so that all sides are progressing toward the final completed design—for a while the cube will look even more disorganized, but in fact all the pieces are coming together nicely. Your life is just like this Rubik's Cube in that once you create an objective, all aspects are impacted—your particular focus may be just the red side (in this case, your desire to create a harmonious family situation).

An Example of the Two-Week Challenge

Let's play out a possible scenario. Say you begin Flow-dreaming to manifest a happy home life because you and your spouse are fighting—or maybe not talking at all anymore:

— After two days of Flowdreaming for ten minutes a day (or ten minutes twice a day if you're up for it), nothing seems to happen. Then on day 3, you're told that you're being laid off at work. You're terrified and angry, but you continue to Flowdream (and even consider writing me a letter to ask why it seems to have backfired and your life feels like it's going to hell instead of improving).

Now, you think, your family situation can only get worse since you'll have the additional stress of being unemployed. But when you Flowdream, you continue to see yourself and your family happy and together, filled with love and communication. You feel how long-standing issues seem to resolve themselves, and you reach agreements and understandings that were way overdue, while feeling relief, happiness, and thankfulness wash over you. Because you're scared about your finances, you add in thoughts that you and your family have all the material comforts you desire and everything is taken care of. (To answer a common question: yes, you can Flowdream about more than one area or thing in your life at a time.)

Imagine the Rubik's Cube turning and turning in the invisible energies. Things are seemingly going more and more out of alignment, even while they are forming into a new, improved, more organized and intended state.

— On days 4, 5, and 6, you're still feeling terrible, and now you and your spouse are fighting about what to do next. Still, you persist in your creative Flowdreaming, feeling good, powerful, and uplifting changes swirl you and your spouse forward into even better things. You may spend a good portion of your day feeling upset, but when you Flowdream, you create raw, forceful emotion that supercedes all other emotions you may have accidentally "broadcast" that day.

— By day 7, you may not know why, but you wake up feeling really good. Even your family seems to be rallying around you.

— At day 10, you realize that you had outgrown your old job, but you would never have willingly made a move because you were afraid of the future and of losing your security. Your spouse is recognizing this as well, and you find that the two of you have actually begun talking because of this unexpected "tragedy." You go a step further in your Flowdreaming and see yourself from your future standpoint looking back on this situation, which your future self laughs about because you experienced a perfect resolution that left you and your mate so happy and on a new road. As your "future self," you radiate these feelings into your Flow.

— On day 11, an old friend reminds you of something you used to do years ago, and you realize that you have a well of potential you'd completely forgotten about.

Now, you want a happy ending to this, right? Let's see.

— On day 12, you and your spouse have a "break-through" conversation—the kind you only have very rarely, where you both say all that you've held in for so long. This conversation happens because you feel that all is so far lost, what with a job loss and possible divorce, that you feel you don't have much left to lose. And so the truth comes out.

— On day 13, you and your mate realize that you still have something together. Your conversation has reminded you of how it used to be before you both became too frightened to share with each other and unable to confess the fear that you were growing apart. And then you explain that you need a new career so you can feel a reason to live. Your spouse accepts this—with all the uncertainty that comes with it—because he or she knows that the "you" of these recent years, while safe and stable, was in essence killing the soul of the "real you."

— Then on day 14, the realization comes that not only has your relationship shifted dramatically, but your job loss was the unlikely catalyst for revealing the antidote to your personal situation. Your Flowdreaming caused an interesting cascade of events, but now both situations that were out of balance—out of Flow—have been set on the correct path. All that remains is fulfillment of the planned desires: a new job in a line of work you love, and to rebuild your relationship now that the old disharmony has been swept away.

Don't stop Flowdreaming on day 14. Instead, recognize that you've initiated a series of events that are still playing out. This "new road" you're on feels easier, more profitable, and more fulfilling and to keep moving down it, you'll want to keep Flowdreaming. It's a little scary and uncertain, as all new things are, but you've set forth the outline for a new set of experiences to encounter, and your Flow is busy arranging them.

This is the power of a two-week challenge. The "challenge," of course, is like one you'd set for yourself at the gym—it's a self-imposed goal meant to prove how you can effectively manifest in your life. The challenge is meant to get you moving on a new path as you define the parameters for the new events and feelings you want to encounter.

When the Challenge Seems to Fail

Occasionally, I receive letters from people who tell me, "I've been Flowdreaming for 30 days now and . . . nothing. Nothing has changed." The implication is that manifesting doesn't work, or that the person is doing it wrong, or that it's in fact working but the person can't see how.

If *you* believe that manifesting doesn't work, then you should just put this book down and take up another art. Or, you can read other people's materials and continue to try to convince yourself of its validity. But if you think you're doing it wrong, you may have a point. For wherever you put your desire, you will see it reflected back in the events and situations that come to you. Perhaps, as I mentioned earlier, you spent all your time pre-acting feelings of *wishing and wanting*, rather than *having and being,* in which case you've manifested more wishing and wanting, right on schedule. (Again, review Emotional States and Their Uses at the back of the book to help you choose the best emotions to use.)

But what if you insist that you do believe in manifesting and are doing it right, but you're still not seeing any results at all? Perhaps the following scenario will help you see why:

Suppose you're trying to Flowdream a new lifestyle in alternative medicine, but your son is addicted to drugs, steals your money, and sets fire to your house. By trying to help him, you've become more focused on involving yourself with *his* Flow, or life experience, than your own. Your goal of practicing alternative medicine has been taken over by your more urgent and stronger emotional response to your son. You didn't choose your son's lifestyle, but you *did* choose to involve yourself with it. Your connection to, and acceptance of, this situation as a part of your life will of course impact all other areas—recall the Rubik's Cube. You can't segment out one part of your life and expect that it won't impact the other areas.

In this case, if your life "isn't changing," it may be because you're refusing to allow the change. You may be resisting reassessing your relationship with your son, so the dream of practicing medicine will continue to remain in the background, no matter how hard you intend it. You're preventing the initial shift of the cube. It's as if you're holding a door shut that leads to a maze of new opportunities.

Look at the obvious: practicing medicine or healing requires a balanced, harmonious life for yourself if you wish to offer healing to others. If you have a condition that needs healing in your own life, that's going to come up first, even if your supposed focus is on "work."

Regarding a family member who's a part of a situation that needs changing, consider that there will always be plenty of other people who want to negatively involve you in their Flows (that is, in their experiences and situations) including loved ones, co-workers, and even strangers. They'll want you to continue to play your part (enabler, money lender, emotional pincushion, you name it). You must learn discretion: be choosy and become willing to change your contribution—your presence—in their Flow so that you can fluidly shift your own direction without being held by ropes and chains to what *they* want you to do or be.

WHAT IF THINGS REALLY ARE CHANGING, but *your awareness* isn't? Sometimes you become so used to your situation that even when new opportunities come, you fail to see or act on them, and life passes by. For example, what if you're given a free ticket to fly to a friend's house across the country, but you think it over until the opportunity passes? Your Flow has brought you something, but you allowed it to pass by unsampled. If you had taken that flight, it turns out that you would have stepped into your Flow and the path of good things coming your way—the woman who would have sat next to you on the plane was looking for a contact just like you to help her business, and away you could have gone into a new financial lifestyle.

Sadly, we think we know when we let something important slip by, but windows often open and close without our even realizing it. That offhand remark you overheard may have stirred an idea in you that would have led you to a new spiritual teacher, but you never made the connection. That storefront you kept driving past—the one your Realtor friend tried to interest you in—is suddenly leased by someone else when it could have become your new restaurant. In other words, you fail to connect the dots, whether from fear or ignorance, and so your Flow continues to labor in finding new things to put before you.

Another classic example of failing to see the opportunities—and changes occurring—before you happens when you become stuck on the minutiae of details. Remember when we discussed knowing what to Flow for and I cautioned you to shoot straight for the emotional end point and allow the details to work themselves out for you? For some people, that's a hard dictum to follow. You put so many conditions on what you want that you keep constricting your goal and pushing it farther out of reach, like squeezing a water balloon with your hands. Every little detail is a "limiter" on your desire.

Let's pretend that you've accomplished something, such as writing a book, and you want the whole world to know about it and enjoy it. Your ultimate goal is to feel extraordinary happiness that so many people read it—along with being validated as a good writer and knowing that you offered a quality, useful book to the world. You also want to feel well compensated for it so that it brings you a nice income. In a nutshell, you feel . . . *happiness* (Yippee! I wrote a book that has been published!), *validation* (and people say it's a well-written book!), *purpose* (I've created something enriching or entertaining and helped others), and *compensation* (I made so much money that I can afford to write more!). These are the four main feelings that come up again and again, in overwhelming intensity, whenever you envision your book in your Flow.

But what if instead of focusing solely on the feelings that the goal of publishing a book creates for you, you instead begin adding limiters? One of these might be your belief that you need an agent, and then a publisher. But you don't want a little publisher; you want a big publisher, and one that gives you an author tour—and you want to be on *Oprah,* and this has to happen by Thanksgiving, and the book cover has to look just so, and you need a certain amount of money as an advance . . . on and on it goes.

What happens is the wide-open directive (happiness! validation! purpose! compensation!) has been more and more restricted by all your beliefs about what precisely is required to get you to those feelings. You have created a bottleneck of energies, and may have inadvertently set up "unflowing" conditions or limitations that your Flow will now have to factor in. Your Flow could and would be changing your life for you, but you keep pruning down the possibilities and then crying, "Nothing's happening!"

Your Flow always knows the easiest way to fulfill your desires . . . if you would only allow it to do its thing, which is to bring you what you ask for in the smoothest, most soul-satisfying way. Your Flow knows how to do this because it's always on track, moving you toward your greatest possible fulfillment. Your Flow is your life unfolding, as pure creation at Source level, and it always knows the quickest, most harmonious way to bring your dreams to life.

The Coin

I often like to pull out the coin analogy. Someone says, "So, all I have to do is wish it and 'attract' it and Flowdream for it, and it will just happen, right?"

And I say, "Are you kidding?" If it were so easy, there would be no reason for me to write this book, or anyone to read it, because we'd all have won the lottery and be sitting on tropical islands.

So I pull out the coin idea: everything you do has two aspects, or two sides. We live in a world of duality, and in everything we look at, we see harmonious opposites. These opposites make a balanced whole, like a coin's heads and tails. Sometimes we see individual situations that are wildly out of balance, but somewhere, somehow the balance is ultimately restored—maybe not in the particular situation you're looking at, but overall.

Nature loves attaining states of equilibrium, which is why we humans often fear change so much. It's our nature to try to keep things just as they are, even when "just as they are" isn't so great. Fear of the unknown always outweighs the resignation of facing more of the crummy known.

On our coin, one side represents our ability to design our interior and exterior world by working with Flow energy. The other side represents the physical action, or *doing* things to get the objects and situations we desire. If you Flowdream without physically acting on tasks aligned with your goal, then nothing happens. You must work toward your Flowdreaming goals if you want to experience their total manifestation in your life. Sometimes this means just being ready for the right opportunity to come up, while other times it means the equivalent of knocking on doors.

However, more often the problem is that people spend far too much time on the "doing" side—the world of material effort—without programming their Flow with their desires. We struggle and plan and act, but we never "check in" to make sure what we're doing is the most effective. We forget to ask, "Is what I'm encountering easy, flowing, and yielding up benefit after benefit, or am I pushing against the current and trying to force a situation that isn't in my ultimate best interest?" It's always a back-and-forth dance between programming and action.

If you want to know just where you are right now in terms of the balance of manifesting and action in your life, again, look at your current circumstances. Your life right now is always a mirror for your current energy landscape. If you're experiencing ease and comfort and joy in an area of your life, you've probably been within your Flow as you pursued the creation of this aspect of your life. Maybe this means you're happily married. It's a good marriage, and you're fulfilled. You're balanced in action and desire. Your marriage is in the Flow.

Maybe you're not happy with your work. You've encountered so many letdowns, so many "almosts." You almost got the good job. You almost had that loan to start your business. You almost had that great business partner. You almost got that bonus or that VC funding. You almost had that paper published. You almost were recognized in your field. You were so close to getting that contract renewed. But you didn't and your satisfaction is waning, or you've never felt satisfied at all. Still, you're working, you have some money and a house. It's not all bad. It just isn't *great*. Your action—or inaction and complacency—is trailing your desire in the Flow.

If you were a leaf in your Flow, you would be spinning in circles, buffeted back by tiny whirlpools, essentially going nowhere. This circumstance is an indicator of being partially within that divine Flow of yourself, and partially pursuing goals that move against your greater self.

Your physical effort must reflect the same strength as your energetic desire. Too much desire with too little material work means that the opportunities slip past. Too much work with too little desire means you risk slipping out of your Flow and being caught in full-blown physical exertion—stumbling in the dark, blinded to the path of ease and light.

The Importance of Easy

Before going after what we think we want, we must ask ourselves, "Is what I'm pursuing ultimately going to make me feel good?" We often go after things because we feel we have to; because that's the way everyone else does it; because in the short-term, it looks good; or because we have wild hopes that are completely outside of the reality. We often want things, get them, and then realize that they're not what we expected after all. In this way, we stay on a treadmill of acquisition but are never really satisfied.

For example, my mom called me a few weeks ago and said, "Someone has asked me if I want to start a coffee shop next to this new restaurant they're opening. Doesn't that sound incredible? How fun!" She wanted to know what I thought.

I reminded her of when I worked in a café as a teenager. When the place was sold, the new owners had to fire a bunch of people and work there themselves for 12 hours a day because they couldn't afford more help. I asked my mother if she thought that she'd enjoy dealing with government regulatory agencies such as OSHA. If she sold beer and wine, would she want to deal with the alcohol permits? And, of course, there would be all kinds of inspections. Along with the money she'd have to take from her retirement funds to open the café, she'd have to hire people and make her employees' schedules, pay them, pay taxes on them, deal with their daily problems, and so on. The coffee part would end up as secondary to being a business owner, and she really just wants to be retired. "Does it really feel in your Flow?" I asked her. "Does this kind of stuff excite you, even if it all happened easily?"

Mom wasn't exactly happy that she'd called for my opinion. But then I told her that she should continue going to *other* people's coffee shops, since sitting and drinking and socializing is the only part she really enjoys. She ended up agreeing with me.

My point is that what we *think* we want, and what *really results* when we get our desires, are often very different. But we can't see this at the time: we lose sight of the broader view and get caught up in short-term goals often meant to just patch up the broken areas in our lives, or get us through a short-term problem, such as paying this month's bills, getting through the cold we caught, finishing school, and so on. Sometimes the going gets grueling as we feel like everything we do is constantly difficult. We moan about how so many things we've tried have fallen apart, and nothing ever works out. We're tired from working so much and from having so many dumb, low-paying jobs. And whenever we do achieve a goal, it doesn't really fix the larger situation.

This again is where the idea of Flow comes in. Your Flow is a monitor, like a runner would wear to monitor his or her heartbeat. Your life, like your heart, has an optimal pace and Flow, and when you're in alignment with this Flow of yours, it's like running with the wind at your back, easing your passage forward. *Life becomes easy.*

The importance of *ease* can't be overemphasized. Ease means that the more effort you put in, the greater the rewards you'll receive, because your Flow is free of obstacles. *All* your energies are yielding benefit after benefit, instead of being tied up in resolving obstacles.

When I was going to college, I remember long stretches when I was tired, overworked, and just ready to be done with it. My feelings were of having pushed myself too hard. I was challenged to the max, but I wasn't obstructed from getting through school. I both worked and went to classes full-time, always had just enough money, did well overall, had a nice condo to live in, and a great boyfriend to support me emotionally. College was challenging, but it was not against my Flow.

This is where you must discern between experiencing "ease" and "effortlessness" and just being lazy. My college years were tough because I pushed myself with 70- and 80-hour workweeks, helping me find my own limits of endurance, like driving a speedboat at top speed in the river of your Flow. It took a lot of work, but whatever work

I put in was rewarded (I won lots of prizes, for instance). *Ease* means that your efforts are rewarded. It's your Flow saying, "Do more of this!"

I don't mean that you'll never encounter problems while living in your Flow, but when you do, you'll find that problems often resolve of their own accord, with minimum effort from you. So when you're deciding on what you want, and preparing to get physically involved in acquiring it, check in with your Flow and affirm your ultimate desire, and for an easy, effortless unfolding of your wish:

I am ready for an effortless life, where all I do is rewarded handsomely. I feel opportunities coming to me now that give me a lifestyle that is easy, loving, and fulfilling. Whatever I do, I discover that it all works out for me, and I am experiencing abundance, harmony, and happiness as a result. I already feel the unfolding of this as it is revealed to me in my life. I am excited about what is coming next, since I know it will be so ultimately fulfilling. And, of course, don't forget to plug in the emotion, emotion, emotion, as you pre-act to all this.

Now, you can apply this to any situation. Your goal is to be *led at all times* to those opportunities and experiences that fulfill the emotional criteria you've laid out: happiness, passion, fulfillment, and so forth. Again, notice how you really don't need to lay out any details at all. The Flow creates such a smooth pathway into new experiences that you just have to say what emotions you expect these experiences to create in you.

When you're in your Flow, you accept that you're already going in a direction that's in support of your happiness, and you can apply all your material effort to whatever opportunities come to you when in your Flow, with very few obstacles or derailments. Keep is *easy.*

Going Against Your Flow

When you're out of your Flow, you may not recognize it instantly, but cumulatively. At first, things just become unsatisfying, and then, things become difficult. The job becomes a nightmare. Your new business can't get off the ground. Your boyfriend goes back to drinking. You fight with your family. Whatever you do just doesn't seem to get you anywhere.

You're a bird trying to fly against the wind, dead set on whatever distant tree you see through the rainstorm, struggling against the currents of your Flow. And yet if you turned around, you'd see a warm, dry tree right in front of you.

But you, stubborn bird, have your eyes set on this *one thing you think you must get to make it all better.* And so you struggle your way toward it for months, even years, and it never works out.

Some people who read this are thinking right now that I've just described half their life. *Just let it go,* I say. What isn't working? Where are you struggling? Just stop that— stop whatever you've been doing and turn around. Let go of it and move in a new direction. Maybe it's your marriage. Maybe it's your job. Maybe it's something else. Whatever it is, it's not in your Flow. If it were, it would've been easy and rewarding.

But then what? you say. Because obviously, you're in a panic about this suggestion.

Then you begin to attune yourself to your Flow. Begin by sensing your Flow and learning to feel that natural, forward alignment that is the powerful force of your life moving forward in perfect syncopation with the universe. Sense this like you're a speeding train and your wheels cling to this track—you're holding on to this Flow. It propels you forward. It's your essence, moving you into all the potential experiences you came here to have. You can have, be, or do anything you want. Just sense your direction, sense this current of immense energy at your disposal, and program in the ultimate emotional feelings you want to create in every area of your life.

For most of us, the feelings are the same, no matter what area of life we're zeroing in on. We want to feel happy, satisfied, fulfilled, valued, excited, and passionate about our work, home, children, family, friends, lovers, and hobbies. Maybe this thing you're letting go of will finally have a chance to "air out" and come back to you in a new guise. Or maybe it will be replaced by something even better than you can now imagine. The point is that we all have areas of our lives where we've slipped away from the inherent smooth reciprocity of our Flow. *How did we do this?* we wonder. It starts with negative emotion.

Negative Emotion

So-called negative emotion is an indicator of fighting against the current or struggling against your Flow. Certain aspects of our lives are filled with negative emotions that tell us that this area of our life is not flowing.

Maybe you began slipping away from your Flow because you were spending too much of your time on the side of the coin that's all about physical doing, with no connection to your Flow, reacting blindly to one situation after another. So, you plowed forward in directions that were entirely against your nature and were far from your easiest, most fulfilling path.

You may have gotten yourself into things that feel difficult to get out of, so you tenaciously cling to them while you keep telling yourself that it will work out eventually. You *are* a stubborn bird, fighting those winds to go in a certain direction because you once thought you saw something there.

If you want to know, right now, exactly where you're going against your own current of being, just look at any relationship or situation you have that's causing you to feel bad in any way. There you are—those are the areas where you've struggled and pushed against your Flow to get something you thought was going to be good for you. But they aren't. Or they once were, but you got yourself stuck, so what was once flowing has now become an anchor in the mud, holding you back. These are the areas to turn around first.

You may wonder, *But I <u>thought</u> it was going to work out, and it didn't. How do I know the difference between what my Flow is and what's just my own stubborn will? Why can't what I want <u>always</u> be in my Flow?*

Here's a rule of thumb: if you desire something and are attempting to obtain it, but from the beginning it's fraught with complications and difficulties, and it continually creates more negative emotion in you, then what you're after isn't in your Flow. It's that simple. It doesn't matter if you have the best intentions or are pursuing the highest goal. *The way you're going about getting what you want is just wrong.* There's probably a way to pursue your goal that's in much greater harmony with your being. *But the way you've currently chosen isn't it.*

Consider this scenario: Pretend that you're in your 60s and want to retire, but you have debt. You recently went through a divorce, and your spouse had the better lawyer, so you're broke. So you took a job (you were grateful that anyone hired you at your age) and go to work every day. But it's miserable, you hate it, and your co-workers don't like you much, either. While your stubborn-bird goal is to make enough money to pay your bills, you came to this conclusion out of desperation. Because you never really paused to consider that you could program the energies of your life to bring you what you really wanted. You just went for the obvious mandate: get a job.

Now let's look at another option for you. You could say, "Well, here I am again, making a fresh start like when I was 21. Except this time, I know a lot more. For instance, I'm really good at helping people get organized and at setting up systems. I wonder if I could learn to work with computers, which is something I could do freelance. Hmm . . . that's a possibility, but let's see what my Flow can lead me to first. My emotional end point is to become debt free, have a comfortable income, and spend my time doing something I enjoy with people I like. My feelings are happiness, freedom from fear, abundance, and enjoying a comfortable retirement." You enter your Flow every day and send out this directive, asking that the best, easiest circumstances come to pass to set all this up.

In the second example, you can see that your goal has always been the same, and being debt free and happy is within your Flow, but the method of fulfilling your goal is what's changed. In the first scenario, you just "got a job"; in the second, you programmed your Flow with an emotional end-point desire, then worked toward that as ideas arrived to support the most flowing method to achieve them. In this way, you'd find work that suits your talents and lifestyle. It would be both easy and challenging (challenging in a fulfilling, energizing way), but you wouldn't encounter many obstacles in pursuit of this goal, because you're in alignment with your Flow.

AT THIS POINT, YOU MIGHT BE WONDERING who or what dictates what's ultimately in your Flow, and what isn't. If this question has crossed your mind, then you'll enjoy the second half of this book, in which we look at the larger forces behind Flowdreaming, which I call "Flowthinking." After you've been Flowdreaming for a while, your entire spiritual understanding may change. I'll share some of these new ideas with you in just a bit.

For now, let me just say that the question of "Who or what decides what's in my Flow, and what isn't?" is inaccurate. Flowthinking suggests that there's no God looking down and directing, "Move this way. Don't go down that road. This is your future." Being a true manifesting practitioner means that *you* direct your life experience, and no one else can decide this for you.

Your Flow is an ever-changing work in progress. It hums with a life that's essentially a collection of your entire consciousness, containing all the experiences you've ever had, and possibly ever will. You are blooming into a new being every moment—the direction of your Flow is always forward and accumulative.

More than just your physical brain, "You" extend deep into awarenesses that you hardly know of in this single, limited physical perspective you're having as a human being. These deeper parts of you have goals and desires as well. If you set forth the desire, *I choose to be fulfilled and loved, and to let go of all my past traumas so I can be emotionally healthy and a powerful creator from now on,* this deeper part of you that I call your "Greater You" can draw from resources you can't even imagine.

Chapter 5

Waiting for Results: The Truth about Manifesting

When will it ever happen? Anyone who has spent time working with the energies of manifesting or the Flow has asked this question. And since I hear this from countless people every week, let's revisit some ideas that I touched on earlier.

When what we want doesn't come quickly, we wonder if we're doing something wrong: maybe we're not Flow-dreaming "correctly." Then we wonder if the whole thing isn't just bogus, since nothing appears to be happening. We get frustrated, but still we long for our objective—and we get angry that we spent time and placed our hopes on something that so obviously hasn't worked.

My friends, always keep in mind that we're each just a babe in the woods in this large and complex world of energy—a web of creation that spans millennia and goes into unknown universes and dimensions of being. Our attempts to harness this energy are like a child attempting to direct a crowded intersection full of traffic. We can't possibly know the millions of small events, precise timing, and perfect synchronicity that goes into the fulfillment of each and every desire put forth. Our job is only to define the experience we wish to have, set the desire into play through our directed Flowdreaming, and then continually reinforce this request through repetition and our confident understanding that we'll receive what we've asked for.

I look at my life on any given day, and I see the analogy of a pear tree. This tree has blossoms, immature fruit, and ripe pears all hanging from its branches. The ripe fruit is what I created for myself through yesterday's thinking. And yet, I deal with those results today—whether they're things I meant to create or not. The immature fruits are the desires that are "in the works," and my newest desires are the small blossoms that will ripen into my physical reality when the time is right and all the correct elements are in play.

Resistance to, and in, the Flow

Everything in your life requires cooperative experiences between people, objects, and situations. Your desire must be *made to order*. This is particularly difficult when you desire something and Flowdream for it, but then it doesn't arrive according to your arbitrary schedule. When this happens, you begin sending out waves of frustration or impatience, but these emotions negate the thing in question. Frustration is an energy that confirms your lack of having. You intend it, and in the next breath, you intend your lack of it. Back and forth, back and forth . . . your desire is caught in a wedge of your own emotional indecision. *It's not here yet* creates more *it's not here yet.*

Sometimes we don't feel frustration, but inadvertently pour in a stealthier cousin: disbelief. When we say to ourselves, "I want a beachfront property in Hawaii and the lifestyle that allows me to enjoy it whenever I want," all kinds of "that's not going to happen for me" reasons float up. We *want* something, but more deeply within us lies a very strong and emotionally well-funded rationale for why we have what we do, and why we can't have more. Part of us is deeply invested in explaining to ourselves why our life is the way it is.

Have you ever spoken to people who say they want to change, but then when you begin helping them, they give you all the reasons why they can't? Why would they defend their own limitations? Sometimes the need to be right, and to justify past decision making, unconsciously outweighs the desire for transformation.

Another emotion—dissatisfaction—also sends out waves of negation. Here is a important point that the novice often misses: *you can desire new things in life without having to feel dissatisfied with what you now have.* If you want a new house, for instance, you don't need to begin by hating the one you live in now. You can instead continue to love your current home, and find all its good aspects that you can. Say to yourself, "I love my home, and I also love my newer, bigger house that is completely paid off, with a huge yard, and lots of sunshine. I continually move toward more and more enjoyment of where I live."

And what about those other emotions: anxiety, panic, neediness? Consider this question that Ann, a listener of my radio show recently sent me:

*I follow the Law of Attraction and have considered
that maybe I'm not "grateful enough" . . . or I'm coming too much from a state of "need." So I work on those
aspects of manifesting, but to no avail! I only wind up
frustrated, confused, and with great feelings of anxiety
and panic, which puts me right back into the consciousness of "need." In Flowdreaming, what part do "gratefulness" and coming from "need" play in manifesting?*

Ann is asking if she's at fault for her lack of success. Of
course she is! If she wasn't, then she wouldn't be the powerful creator that she is. She already knows that when she
needs something, she's just sending out confirmation that
she lacks it. By doing this, she's creating more neediness,
not fulfillment. *She's pre-acting her future need.*

What about being grateful? Well, let's turn that into
appreciation instead. Gratefulness can trigger an association
in some of us with the feeling of being given something,
or rewarded, by a greater power. It makes us dependent on
someone else's good humor to fulfill our desires. Appreciation, on the other hand, is a much more neutral feeling.

However, the core of this question is Ann's self-doubt.
What I really hear Ann saying is, "I don't have faith in my
ability to manifest. Am I good enough to do this? Or is my
thinking so rotten that I just can't get past it?"

Flowdreaming is a potent skill. It's concentrated—much
like that laundry detergent where you only need to use
a capful. Just a few minutes of Flowdreaming counter-
balances almost all the other thoughts and feelings you
continuously pour out during the day—that's what's so
magnificent about it.

You'll probably continue to worry about, obsess over, and be frightened of those parts of your life that aren't working. You know you need to change your thinking, but that's easier said than done. You'll feel negative emotion, then you'll feel guilty that you felt it, in a self-perpetuating cycle. But when you're Flowdreaming, you're rebalancing the energetic scales. Flowdreaming paves over that constant stream of doubt, like pouring thick blacktop over a bed of restless leaves. It's concentrated energy work, and if done often enough, it will override all that negative programming that you continue to pour out.

As humans, we worry; that's built into us and we can't stomp it out. Isn't is nice, though, that we've evolved a compensating factor, like Flowdreaming? When we Flowdream, we offset our worry with our real, much more powerful desires. The power of our Flow is awesome and highly corrective. It atones for all those other feelings.

So what if Ann's sense of panic or doubt surfaces when she's Flowdreaming? I find that when people feel resistance in their Flow, it could very well mean that the Flow is telling them something.

Often, it's your Flow saying, *That direction, that desire, is not in harmony with your greater, overall self. You're trying to shove a square peg in a round hole.* Other times, your Flow is simply revealing your current energy state: it shows you what fearful or despondent feelings you've been filling your energy field with. For example, you may enter your Flow and see yourself riding an escalator and the more you try to climb, the more it takes you downward. In other words, if you've been loading up on guilt, sadness, anxiety, or pessimistic thinking, then your Flow will reflect that back at you because you put it there. Similarly, if you see something blocking you or barring your way, such as a dam, the Flow is simply showing you the resistance you've built up to your desire.

Since your Flow is always in motion, it creates your future moment by moment. It's like standing on a road watching it being built in front of you, one foot at a time. So if you encounter fear, doubt, or resistance in your Flow, simply say, "Thank you for revealing my current state to me. Now, as I move forward, I feel all this fear releasing itself from me, flowing away behind me. It seeps like a gray haze out of me and swirls away, gone. I feel myself becoming lighter and more buoyant as I'm released to shoot forward in my life."

By doing this, you're creating a new pattern for release that will continue to help you move away from old feelings you no longer want. The Flow never carries resistance as part of its nature. Resistance, fearful imagery, or any discordant emotion has always been put there *by your own thinking,* never by Source.

ANOTHER FEELING WE OFTEN ENCOUNTER in our Flow is that we *don't deserve* what we ask for. (I could write a another book just on this!) Even though we might desperately desire something, another part of ourselves feels as though there are reasons why we shouldn't have it. We say to ourselves, *I didn't work for it. I didn't go to school for it. My parents never had this. Am I good enough to have this in my life? Someone else is smarter, wealthier, handsomer, healthier, more interesting, funnier, more attractive, has had more experience, has a better resume, has better connections,* and on and on. We invent reasons in our mind why someone else is more deserving than us, while convincing ourselves to settle for less.

My friends, this is crucial: No one is more worthy than you to have, be, or do anything you want. We all come here as equal parts of Source, or God, energy. Each of us is as deserving as anyone else.

Feeling undeserving is a crutch that we use to justify to ourselves why we can't have something. It's a crippling feeling. The wealthiest man, the most successful woman— none of them are inherently more deserving than you to have what they have. God doesn't favor one person over another.

As you Flowdream, you may feel resistance in the form of inadequacy. This feeling of *I'm not good enough* or *I don't deserve this* may manifest itself in you in many ways: as a nagging worry while you're in your Flow, an inability to stay focused, an inability to really feel yourself having and being what you want, or as a feeling of *But how . . . ?* Fill in the blank with any justification you may have for why you can't be happy or why what you ask for just can't come true.

It's important to recognize when you're feeling undeserving and begin to Flowdream (and pre-act) the opposite. Say to yourself instead, "I am incredibly deserving to have this or become this. I am as deserving as anyone else on this Earth. We all come here for our own special set of experiences here in life, and there is no reason in the world why I shouldn't have mine. If I give up my place in line to have this, someone else will gladly take it! So why can't that person be me? We are all equally deserving. I am a good, loving person and the Universe knows this, and my Greater Self knows this, and I am deserving of the best that life has to offer."

Facing your feelings of inadequacy, and overcoming them, will help you immensely in your manifesting. If you've been Flowdreaming toward something for a long time and it hasn't happened yet, take the time to ask yourself if you've been simultaneously flooding your Flow with thoughts of not being good enough to have what you asked for. If you have, you can clearly see how you've been both creating *and* negating all this time. Spend time in your Flow feeling nothing but utter entitlement for a while. Feel how brilliant, talented, lovable, and healthy you are. Remind yourself that no one else is like you, and no one is inherently better. All snowflakes are beautiful and perfect in God's eyes. We *are* all created equal.

Understanding Cycles

Sometimes what you want doesn't arrive on your arbitrary schedule because you're caught up in what I call a "cycle."

If we keep with the analogy of the Flow as a river—and you're part of this river—then notice how easily your whole life moves forward at times, bringing many harmonious events. You might tell yourself that all your planets are lined up just right, or your hard work is finally paying off. One good situation seems to bring another, and you start to feel as if all the pieces are finally coming together. During these periods, or cycles, we're at ease with the world, and whatever we do tends to go in our favor.

However, at a certain point, the wind shifts. For any one of a thousand reasons, we encounter an obstacle in our life, and as we begin to obsess over it, we've metaphorically turned within our Flow and begun pushing against it.

Swimming upstream is hard. Laborious. And what's more, for all the effort you put in, there seems to be no result. At best, you're treading water. This may be related to a new career you're trying to launch, or to a relationship that has gone awry. Maybe you and your mother are fighting all the time. Maybe your family has erupted with strife and anger. Maybe you've developed an illness. Maybe you've put on weight. Maybe you're experiencing an inner crisis, crippled by the feeling that life is passing and you have yet to make your mark. Yet the more energy you put into your situation, the worse it gets.

What's more, you begin to notice as the weeks, months, or even years wear on, that other areas of your life become ensnared in this mess. You lose your job. You fight with your roommate or spouse. Your car breaks down. You keep choosing friends who betray your trust. Every area of your life becomes caught in this same wrong direction. You're not only feeling disconnected from your Flow, but you wonder if there even *is* such a wonderful place, because for all your trying, you accomplish nothing.

This cycle is the opposite of Flow. You're experiencing struggle or apathy because it seems like whatever you do, nothing seems to change. Eventually, you get tired—tired of life—or even depressed.

Breaking a Negative Cycle

Like that exhausted swimmer, you realize that your efforts are getting you nowhere. But, if you still think your goals are really what you want, now is the time to choose another cycle—one of repair. In this cycle of energy, turn your attention away from fighting your problems head-on. Instead of pursuing the same paths you have been, pause and reevaluate your goals. Then reevaluate your methods to achieve those goals, because something you're doing is clearly against your own inner rhythm.

I live in California near the ocean, where we often have a dangerous swimming condition called a riptide. In a riptide, an undertow pulls you out into the ocean instead of pushing you toward the shore. These rip currents overpower swimmers and can pull them out for miles, and there's no fighting against them. People *drown* when they try to swim against this current toward the shore. The only way out is to begin swimming parallel to the shore— sideways. Although it's counterintuitive since you aren't heading back to the safety of land, it's your only choice in order to remove yourself from the rip current.

This is a perfect example of how I change cycles in my life. When I'm in a cycle that causes suffering, I first work backward to see if I can identify the cause that pulled me from my Flow. There's always a trigger, and sometimes it can seem completely neutral. It doesn't appear to be anything of consequence, except that it represents a disruption in my Flow that pulls me into negative-reaction mode. For instance, did I get ill or run down or stressed? Was there something about my work that was making me feel upset? Am I fighting with a friend or family member, and not connecting about something critical in our lives? Am I upset about something and putting on weight instead of facing it?

Let's take a look at a longer scenario, and try to identify the initial trigger that provoked this person's negative emotions and pulled them from their Flow. Say I've started a massage practice, but it isn't working out. I paid the rent for a space, then found out it was drafty and noisy, and now I can't get my money back. Plus, there's a masseur in the area who's been undercutting my price and taking my clients. So I began arguing with the landlord and am now threatening to sue him. I'm so depressed that my boyfriend and I have started fighting; because I've become so short-tempered, his formerly mildly annoying habits have suddenly become really, really irritating. In short, I tried to do something that I thought was in my Flow, but it just seemed to get thrown back at me until everything in my life got disrupted.

Let's work it backward: I want to start a massage practice, but now all my attention is taken up with damage control. I'm in reaction mode, clearly swimming against my Flow in this situation. I think about it, and discover that I'm really just trying to do something for money, but I really don't care about massage. I'd much rather counsel people nutritionally, but I can't afford the schooling. Or, maybe I *do* love massage, but I was only renting the space because it seemed like a good deal. I'd much rather work in a large spa, but the pay was worse so I regretfully decided not to.

Do you see the trigger, where I veered away from the path of ease, the path of my original desire that may have been most fulfilling, because I allowed my fears to take over? My Flow gave me the gift of *resistance* to try to turn me around and move me back to my original desire. It tried to show me, "Don't rent this place, because you don't really want to be here." I didn't listen, so it kept giving me continual resistance until I got the message: turn around and try a different path.

At this point I need to stop swimming against my current and break this cycle. I must begin swimming sideways—stopping whatever I was doing that was getting me nowhere. Instead of doggedly trying to fix this situation, I should focus on the initial resistance I encountered, and move in another direction. In this case, I could ditch the space I'd rented and decide to go to clients' homes, or I might talk to that beautiful day spa after all about renting a room there. In other words, I ought to examine other avenues that are more in keeping with my Flow. *Same goal, new route.* And it's vital that I remember to focus on my emotional happiness in the end—how I want to end up feeling—so then the path there will *define itself* for me.

If you try something, it works, and you feel good as a result, then you're experiencing a path of energy in harmony with yourself. If you try something and you're obstructed, nothing happens, or you feel upset, then you're going in the wrong direction and should change routes. Notice that I don't advocate "giving up." A goal has more than one path to achieving it. Seek the one that keeps you in a good cycle, that works with the whole of your life, and that's in harmony with who you are.

Too often we cram ourselves into paths of achievement that others have outlined for us. For instance, sometimes we have to take that predefined path by getting a diploma from a college or university. But even there, we have many choices: where to go to school, or how (in person, online, four-year university, community college, and others). The point is that we grab on to what others or our first instinct tells us we must do, and never stop to evaluate if it would be good for us, or if there is a better, faster, easier way to accomplish our goal.

It's much better to find a method for getting what you desire that works within your overall picture—your life's Flow—by asking yourself what will make you truly happy. And we must task our Flow, before starting out, to bring us only the best circumstances and choices to pick from. Oftentimes you might think you want something, but that greater part of you knows that it's less than ideal. In this case, let go of the desire, cast it into your Flow, and say,

"I choose to find work [or what have you] that is wonderfully fulfilling, in which I'm surrounded by people who love me and admire what I do, and in which I feel satisfied that I've done something worthwhile." Then allow your Flow to bring you your request as defined by your overall criteria above. This is powerful manifesting because you're acknowledging that in your limited perspective, you don't know all the career possibilities that you could encounter; instead, you're putting your trust in a higher level.

Like a swimmer in a riptide, once you learn to stop and "swim sideways" for a while, then you can make your way to shore and into a new cycle.

Short Cycles

Cycles seem to have a Flow of their own. As people, we are continually interacting with the Flows of others and the Flows of things such as businesses, schools, and even economies. Everything has a Flow of being, an energy signature, not just people. When we live in a community, we're subject to the energy conditions of that place. If our town has lost jobs and a lot of people are in despair, then that's a Flow of energy like anything else. It permeates the area, and influences our own Flows as well.

Imagine yourself as a little current of water inside a much larger river. What affects the people and places you interact with, affects you. If your family is negative and fights with each other, and you choose to be with these people, you too accept the "negativity" of this current. A family in a cycle of arguing carries you in this cycle.

Cycles don't have to be long; sometimes they can be as short as a day or just a few hours in which everything you encounter might be either nettlesome or profoundly synchronistic and joyful. But the nettlesome cycles tend to be noticed more—which is often your impetus to Flowdream. In this kind of aggravating cycle, you bicker with family and co-workers. People on the road get mad at your driving. Someone steals your parking spot. Your best blouse gets a coffee stain. You have a scratchy throat. You can't reach any people on your "to call back" list. Only the most expensive plumber in town is available to fix your sink, which of course just broke. All this happens in a matter of hours or a day or two.

You must break this short cycle—it doesn't matter what triggered it—and you can easily do so with a small trick. First, you must find a way to pause and remove yourself from this "small Flow" of discord you've accidentally dipped into, and this will break your attachment to it. I do this all the time. Usually, I find myself sitting in a parking lot, frustrated and angry, and I look at my to-do list and say, "Sorry, that's it. I'm going home. I'm going to have a cup of tea and sit in the sun, so all of this can wait until the cycle passes." I just completely stop what I'm doing.

Or if I'm at work, I put on my running shoes and walk around the business park while Flowdreaming, feeling all the stress melting off and trailing away behind me—the cycle dissipating and disappearing.

You'll find that all the plans you put together during a cycle like this are likewise "corrupted" in some way. Don't bother calling it Mercury retrograde: call it a cycle. So call back the plumber and cancel, or throw away the blouse and write it off as a loss. Do what you can to "undo" the previous cycle so it doesn't *cling* to you. Move sideways out of it by not focusing on any of the things you'd previously intended to do during the next few hours or that day. Your intention to accomplish certain things preceded you, and by stepping out of this intended route, you force the energies to reorganize on the fly into something else.

Long Cycles

What about cycles that seem to last for months and don't appear to be attached to anything? When everyone else around you is doing well, your town is doing well, and you're the only one who isn't?

Again, pinpoint the trigger for this cycle if you can. If that's not possible, consider the idea that your life Flow has its own inner rhythm. Like our sleep cycles, there are periods of activity and rest in our Flow. We may move for years at a high rate, accomplishing goals and really squeezing the juice out of life. And then . . . the doldrums hit; we're in a rut. Years go by when nothing seems to happen, like a boat drifting aimlessly in a pond.

I've experienced that my Flow has high spots and low spots, times of rest and times of activity. In the active times, I may really be enjoying lots of experiences, reaping rewards, and creating and manifesting with abandon. And then . . . nothing. No change. Whatever I try just peters out. I feel like I'm knocking my head against a wall. Am I out of my Flow? No. My life remains fairly stable and full. Good things of small consequence happen to me. But, *I* feel bored. I feel restless. I feel like the new things I want to create and manifest go nowhere, like a stream drying up on desert sand.

Any physicist can tell you that energy is transmitted in waves, and a *sine curve* is a representation of that wave. A wave has peaks and troughs, mimicking those of our own sleep/wake rhythm, and of the cyclical nature of life itself—moving as it does between birth, death, and rebirth, as energy recycles itself again and again into new forms. Peaks and troughs. The wave that crashes onto the shore is pulled back out to sea.

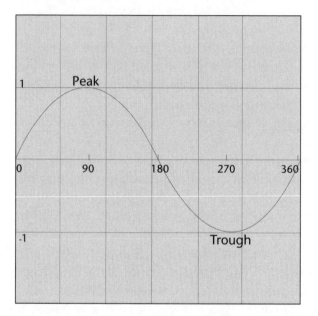

I still encounter these troughs, or lulls, with some frustration, but I'm getting better at dealing with them. I remind myself that just as my body rests, so does my life energy, as it follows its optimal waves through life. When I'm in a rut, I endeavor to feel a graceful acquiescence as I look at what this low point brings. As with the ocean surf, when the tide is low, a new landscape emerges. All kinds of previously hidden shells and small animals can be seen. It's a time for quiet exploration. Those of you familiar with tarot would call this "the Hermit Card." If you have a religious background, you may call it "the dark night of the soul"—a time of reflection, spiritual crisis, or a period of self-realization. It's a time for making plans, shifting values, or examining your current life. It may be a long cycle.

Our lows can feel endless. Years will pass while we look at everyone who seems to be getting farther ahead than we are—going to great places and doing exciting things with their lives. Their careers are booming and families are growing, while we wait for something to happen or for a situation to work itself out. Keep in mind that times of reflection and slower development are crucial for effective Flowdreaming. We can't always try to rush ahead, thinking it will force us out of a lull—after all, even racehorses get winded.

I remind myself that I'm not in a competition with anyone or climbing any ladder. If I have time to sit in the sunshine Flowdreaming because nothing else has worked out for my day, I feel thankful that I have the time and peace to line up all the possibilities of my existence.

My goals are to develop a life that pleases me in every aspect. I want fulfillment in every way, and I'm free to explore any new cycles of experience that I think will take me closer to that goal. So if I take a month, a year, or more to reemerge into the active wave of my Flow, I'll use this time to explore the depths of the trough. I will see it as an opportunity.

For me, years like this have made me realize the importance of my family, in particular how good it feels to give my children time and attention as they grow. It has made me examine what my real goals are as I take the time to consider what all the dead ends I've encountered really mean.

Time to do nothing but reflect is actually a treasure. And, although you might say, "But I'm tired of reflecting about my dead-end job and coming home to an empty house," this period, like all phases, will come to an end.

Oddly enough, we usually emerge from these low points without even realizing it. One day we're down, and then the next we're up, as if we were slowly being lifted higher and higher, until suddenly we notice the new, high, bustling view.

Chapter 6

Default Mode, Desire, and Ego

As you learned from the last chapter, if you've been wanting to fix an area of your life for years, and yet it always remains the same, you might be in a cycle or you might simply have been struggling against your Flow, year after year. When you don't learn how to break free from (or at least work with) your cycles or learn to turn away when you encounter resistance, and realign yourself with you Flow, you may start looking for things to blame your circumstances on. That's exactly the kind of thinking that robs you of your power to change.

You might say, "It's my fate/my destiny/karma/God's will/my life lesson/my astrological sign/my family's fault/ the result of my screwed up childhood that my life is *always* like this." But whenever you assign your situation to the machinations of a source outside of your creation, you hand over your ability to manifest.

If you think that karma leads you to an unhappy love life, for instance, then this mysterious force will always have power over you. You're saying that your happiness is dependent on something outside yourself and your control, and things won't improve for you until this force allows them to.

If you blame past lives for an unhappy relationship, you and your lover may in fact be energetically tied together in a way that extends into deeper energies, but you're not in a straightjacket set of circumstances in which you deserve a punishment or rebalancing. In other words, while you might have past interactions with this person, and the universe does trend toward seeking balance, you are a fluid, adaptable creature. You can respond in any way to the choices ahead of you or move in any direction at any moment, so if you choose to submit to some idea of punishment or retribution, then that's the experience you're seeking.

The real problem is that we usually respond to situations the same way, all the time. We create habitual patterns of interaction with everything around us, and one of those is that we don't consciously *manifest* (or pre-act)—we *react*, blindly accepting whatever comes our way. So as *recipients* rather than *creators* the majority of the time, we are almost always in what I call *default mode,* but this isn't necessarily bad.

Default Mode

Default mode is where we spend 99 percent of our time. It's the "baseline" of our life and the level that all experiences fall into, like water finding equilibrium. If a person's default mode is quite high, then they appear "successful." In reality, that person's default mode has a certain "more pleasurable" set of parameters laid in—they manifest more money, for example, because they can't imagine doing otherwise. Or, a person manifests wellness because in their mind, they've "always been really healthy."

Our default mode is a combination of our expectations and the manifesting we're always doing without being aware of it. Much like autopilot, our default mode automatically limits certain experiences, and accepts others, without our even being aware of this.

Even when it's unacknowledged, we're always creating and sending out the programming for "what happens next." Think of default mode as the general underlying set of restrictions or requests that we have in our lives for the kinds of circumstances that come to us. It's built of our behavioral patterns, assumptions, unspoken beliefs, subconscious choices, and unconscious acceptance of others' "Flow requests" that come into our experience—whatever guides us in all experiences and encounters when we're not manifesting consciously. In other words, it's what's there when we are not paying attention and are just dealing with life. Our lives right now probably reflect our unconscious default mode, unless we've been practicing Flowdreaming or manifesting for some time and actively working with the energies to request newer, better experiences.

You may have a default mode that's less than pleasurable. If flies are buzzing en masse outside your house, it's as if you don't have window screens. You take in and deal with *everything* that flies your way. A conscious Flowdreamer, however, puts up screens that filter out what isn't wanted. How defined your screen is explains your default mode. When you don't consciously define that screen, it's as if your eyes are closed, and you're stumbling through life, accepting whatever it throws at you. In fact, every person you encounter has a million ways for you to become engaged with their Flow, their lives, their dramas—and you're continually being invited in.

Consider this: If you have a Flow, so does everyone around you. And we're here to interact with each other because we all need participants. And every time you accept an "invitation" to have an engagement of one type or another with someone, you are, for the duration of the encounter, accepting that person's Flow into your own, like two small streams merging, then disengaging when your joint experience is over.

Thanks to your current default mode, you may have accepted interactions with many people whose Flows are strewn with boulders and debris, challenges and disharmony. You've taken their problems in when you've engaged in a Flow jointly with them.

For example, when you're a victim of road rage, you're "pulled in" temporarily to another person's overwhelming anger. Your stomach knots up and you feel upset and angry. Your Flow met theirs and didn't like what it felt. But when someone gives you a sincere compliment, your Flow and theirs are in harmony, and it feels great.

Habitually interacting with people, jobs, or lifestyles in which there's turmoil, anger, ambiguity, or hopelessness also impacts the default mode of your Flow. Have you sunk to the level of everyone around you through your inattention? If so, you're not looking at a cycle—you're looking at a climb toward greater awareness and direction as you begin working with your Flow to find a default mode that more closely resonates with you.

Your default mode can be a great source of power for you. It can contain "rules" that limit and define what generally enters your life. Such a default mode would contain such directives as:

- *Whenever choices come to me, I'm always led to the one that's for my greatest good and happiness.*

- *Whenever I stray from my Flow, I'm never gone long, since my Flow always nudges me back.*

- *I never have to worry about going off in the wrong direction since its assured that I'll be guided back to ease and happiness in all things.*

- *I don't have to be afraid to make important decisions, because even if I'm wrong, my Flow will bring in the easiest solutions to put me on the right course again.*

- *My Flow is always offering up experiences that I'll enjoy and that will make me feel good.*

- *I'm always led toward good health and appreciated in whatever I do.*

- *I always have love in my life.*

Think of your default mode as the general guidelines that your Flow works within. What are yours? Begin to define and be aware of them in every situation of your life, and you'll see the difference.

Speaking of defining your default mode, there's one more thing: it's sometimes shaped by what I call *glass ceilings*. (Please note that I don't use this term in the traditional sense but rather to refer to unseen beliefs that limit almost every human being.)

Glass Ceilings and Limiting Beliefs

Last night I dreamed that I was watching the construction of my perfect home. It was on a golf course—which I was surprised about, since neither my husband nor I golf.* I remember turning back to look at the house, worrying about all the water the grass would consume and thinking about putting down rock instead. The house had a wonderful front yard, a long driveway, and lots of room inside. I worried that the painters would mix up the wall colors in the rooms if I didn't supervise them.

It was a positively mundane dream, but that's what made it so *real*.

I've been working on manifesting a perfect home for several years now, and I'm a little surprised that it's taken this long. But as I continue to think about it, what I've come to understand is that my desires for this home have always been changing.

At first, my highest priority was lots of land and a short drive to work. Whether the house was new, old, or a fixer-upper didn't matter. Then I decided that I wasn't interested in remodeling and wanted the place that was already near perfect. Next I began considering the school district, and this led to a conflict in my mind because the newer residence with lots of land, close to work, was going to be incredibly expensive once I added in the great-school-district factor.

Okay, since I'm manifesting, money should be no object, right?

Except my practical side was screaming, *Where are you going to get the couple of million for this house, especially since you want it paid off, or at worst, only a 15-year mortgage?*

---

*Since writing this passage a year ago, I've since taken up golfing. Funny how the Flow works, offering prescient glimpses of the future.

Because I've been blessed with a rising income year after year and my Flow has continually steered me toward success, I *should* feel confident that I will someday have this house. But it appears that I've hit the ceiling of my beliefs because despite the obvious evidence to the contrary, *I still cling to a limiting belief* that tells me that I've overshot what I believe is affordable or realistic. So whenever I Flowdream about my perfect home, I encounter resistance within myself that reminds me of the *enormity* (which is a code word for "difficulty") of my request and thus the impossibility of manifesting it. Spending several million dollars *is* above my comfort level right now, but that's because I'm thinking narrowly and forgetting about all the ways my Flow can fulfill my desire if I'd just let it get about its work lining up the right situations to bring this house into my life.

Instead of pre-acting my strong, confident trust that this is happening, I've been pouring all my insecurities and worries into my Flowdreaming because I have a glass ceiling of disbelief. Further, what I've been asking for has continually changed, so my "compass" of desire is always swinging from one direction to another.

I share this with you because it perfectly illustrates how a combination of effects can add up to a deadlock in your manifesting life. Even I, as an experienced manifesting practitioner, still find myself facing the same issues as anyone else: inconstancy, doubt, resignation, and lack of belief (despite evidence in front of my nose that should help me see clearly). I have a glass ceiling—an invisible barrier in my mind that limits me, and this leads to paralysis—not just within the energies but in my actions to get the house as well. I've been like a mouse running back and forth in a box under a low plate of glass with the cheese on top, wanting to get the prize above me, but unable to fathom the thing holding me in place. Now that I see my glass ceiling, I can make changes in both the energies and in my physical efforts, where I've also held myself back.

You see, I've been taking weekend drives around town for about two years now, checking out what's for sale. A few weeks ago, I realized that I had no plan put together should I actually find this dream house—I had no preapproval for a loan and no Realtor chosen to sell my current place. I was living in fantasy, all the while moaning and whining about how I can't find or afford the perfect home.

I've now decided to finally tackle this by working from both the physical and energetic ends. I'm looking for loan approval and calling a Realtor to help my husband and me. And from the energetic side, I'm going to once again create my list of priorities for this house, and then I'm going to have a showdown with my feelings of doubt. Most important, I have to understand my ceiling of belief . . . and then I need to raise it.

I talk a lot about limiting beliefs, or glass ceilings, and overcoming these restraints was a central focus in my last book, *The Flowdreaming Prosperity Challenge.* We all create what we consider to be the limits of what's "practical" in our lives and unknowingly put ceilings up for ourselves which are often a pastiche of our family's beliefs, our insecurities, and our self-doubts. So when I say to myself, "Things would have to radically change for me to be able to afford this! How could I even pay the electric bill on a house this big!" what I'm really communicating is, "In my life, I have somehow made myself believe the idea that my husband and I are stuck within our income bracket. There's no way that new sources of money can come to us easily and comfortably. Since I presently don't see any way to afford this home, I should scale down my desire into something more reasonable but less satisfying. Because I feel frustrated and dissatisfied, and I'm packing a lot of emotional energy behind these feelings, I'm unintentionally sending out a continuous stream of manifesting energy that continues to pull to me more situations to support my frustration and dissatisfaction." Even my potent Flowdreaming hasn't been enough to tip the scales, since my desires have been so muddied and I've failed to support it with enough physical action (like getting a Realtor!).

My situation clearly shows how our irrational glass ceilings keep us right where we are. I'm now choosing to work with mine, and to change it (raise it!) so that I can move on. Keep in mind that even when I do move my ceiling up eventually, it will still remain at some other, for the moment unforeseen, level. I'll no doubt encounter it again when I begin to Flowdream for something even better— say, a second home in the Caribbean. If part of me starts kicking and screaming, I'll know I'll have reached my new, higher limit of thinking, and a new glass ceiling will be revealed.

WHEN PEOPLE ASK ME WHY what they're working to manifest isn't coming to them, it can be hard to communicate all the variables that are leading to their unhappiness. As explained earlier, there can be a complex web of feelings involved that create the ceilings that hold us in familiar territory. And it's easy to justify these ceilings by saying, "I'm just being realistic," which is an excuse for why you can't have, be, or do more with your life.

Yes, being practical or realistic is intelligent when it means, for instance, not spending your way into debt. If you outspend your current resources, you're creating a model for the energies that reinforces "more of the same," and you create more situations that encourage overspending. When you spend *within* your resources, you again are setting up an energy pattern of "more of the same." So if your resources aren't enough, work to *increase your resources,* then spend within that.

The other kind of "practical" I'm talking about is the excuses we give ourselves for the dissatisfaction we feel in our present situations. These excuses seem so reasonable and rational to us: "I can't quit my job to become a travel writer because I have a family to support," or "I have to stay married because nobody would hire me and I couldn't support myself on my own."

We, without fail, nail the lids onto our own coffins. And when we begin manifesting, we start to encounter these lids, or glass ceilings, only when, surprised, we bump up against them. What happens is that we begin to desire something and then we begin to work on attracting that something into our lives through our Flow, and then suddenly we feel negativity, frustration, and disillusionment. We pout, "I'm not getting what I want!"

And that's when you need to step back and find out what competing belief is holding you in place. Because it's there, I know.

I've been giving a lot of thought to how our glass ceilings get there in the first place. I don't think we consciously build them; rather, they slip into place over the years, based on erroneous thinking we pick up from the people around us.

If your old schoolteacher gave you only *C*'s, perhaps you thought, *I must not be very smart,* or when you finished high school and went to work, you could have believed, *Well, I wouldn't have finished college anyway.* Now that you're stuck in a job you hate, living all alone in a home you rent, and feeling as if nothing will change, maybe you've started to look back on these thoughts that you acquired from the old situations, and you've looked up and bumped your head on the glass ceiling that you constructed. You may be in a new place in your life, but you're continually running the thinking of those old situations, staying right where you are.

I come to every glass ceiling in my life with a sense of tremendous relief because it reveals something hidden about myself—now that I can see it, I can deal with it. I can work through the loop in my mind that tells me I can't afford the house of my dreams, for example. *Making* a plan isn't all that hard. *Doing* the plan takes effort, and for me, that means letting go of the "But how?" questions in my head and overcoming the fears of how my perfect home will come into being. It means focusing concentrated emotion on the feeling of enjoying this house, and on how I can laugh and dance when the mortgage bill comes because it's so tiny. It's no small task working through this glass ceiling so that I can truly offer my Flow what I desire. I have to imprint these feelings into the energy of my life so that my Flow has the goal clearly laid out for it. I don't need to hassle myself with the "hows"—that's my Flow's job.

Desire with Direction

What about the days when we feel as rudderless as a rowboat? Some days, months, or even years, we simply have no direction. We don't *know* what we want and we wonder what's wrong with us. It's not depression—we just lack any enthusiasm for the buffet of life. It's a fine distinction.

I know this feeling well, as I realized that I'm the kind of person who's always wanting something new. I get tired of what I'm doing after a while and begin to feel restless. But what do I *want?*

This part of my nature came into focus for me when I realized that this quality isn't exactly stellar for building a career. To become good at something, you need to stick with it. Getting bored and fidgety means that you tend to want to jump around a lot. When I accomplish something—even something as big as building the Hay House Radio Network from the ground up, as well as running the audio and video production division of this international company—my next thought is to wipe the dust from my hands and say, "Next!" Once I attain success at something, I immediately want to move on to bigger and better things. Maybe you recognize this tendency in yourself.

So here I am, feeling the need for a new horizon, yet completely without desire as to the direction. Desire, as you're coming to see, is the impetus for the Flow. Desire is the emotion that you're given so that you can create with joy and abandon in this world. Desire is what propels God's experience of Itself through your eyes. In your Flow, you might sense a lack of desire as a sort of standstill—floating without going anywhere. It's different than being in a rut, in which you feel frustration with your lack of progress. It's just a feeling of boredom with all your present options.

And that's exactly what you need: *new options to choose from.* I'll always remember one startling image that came to me years ago in my Flow. I sensed myself standing at the end of a long, dark hall. From my vantage point, all I could see was a blank wall straight ahead, which represented my current state of opportunity. I began to walk down this hall, and as I did, my perspective changed. I began to see that I was passing doors hitherto obscured by my prior perspective, and at the end of that hall were new paths opening on either side of me. I quickly realized that this image was meant to remind me that my current point of view was severely limited.

Now, you can't always know what to ask for when you can't see the options. But as you realize your own limited viewpoint, acknowledge that as you continue to move forward day by day—changing, growing, and experiencing—you'll encounter new experiences and opportunities. One may thrill you. It's unknowable now, but it will reveal itself in your journey.

If you look back on your life, you'll see all kinds of such fortunate coincidences in your "destiny": you landed jobs through lucky breaks or met your life partner when you weren't looking for a relationship. While there are some goals you've worked hard for and achieved, others fell to you without much effort at all. I encourage you to revel in both types of experience—those tried for and those that fell to you—because this offers you a balance of experiences.

The Benefits of the Ego

We can't go any further without pausing now to talk about ego, since for so many people, ego is the same thing as desire. Letting go of ego is letting go of desire, which leads toward bliss—or so we're taught.

When we think of the ego, many of us immediately think of a hostile foe, since that's what it's come to mean in 20th-century society. A mishmash of half-understood philosophies have combined to create a monster for us to master. The ego, we're told, is what gets in our way. It causes us pain, and is responsible for vanity, pride, and selfishness. Freud wasn't keen on the ego, Buddhists seek to move beyond it, and metaphysical teachers speak of it like an evangelist speaks of the devil.

What we call the ego has become a grab bag for all the unpleasant characteristics we see in ourselves. If we're hurt, it's the *ego* that won't let go. If we're angry, it's the *ego* that's been inflamed. It makes us *want things,* and has become the trash heap for our darkest impulses.

So why, then, does the ego not bother me?

Everything in creation serves a purpose, so all things in existence can claim their own right to exist. There is nothing inherently inside me that I would abolish. I might wish to eliminate a nasty flu bug, or to subsume a desire to lash out at someone when I become angry about something, but my ego came with me, as part of my vibration of being, and I want to know what it's doing for me.

What I've found is that ego is more than a collection of our worst impulses. To use myself as an example, I'm often envious of others' successes, I get angry about getting slighted, and I think that I can do things better than other people. I've got three of the seven deadly sins covered here: *envy, anger,* and *pride.* These are uncomfortable parts of my personality that help create unique situations for me. I *could* call all these less-than-charming traits the result of my ego. But instead I'm going to look at them for just what they are—crummy parts of my personality—because at heart, I feel really uncomfortable with the idea that any of us should hate any part of ourselves.

So I have some icky parts in my character—must I despise myself for that? Or can I learn to work with those parts, to mitigate them and keep them in check so I don't hurt myself or others around me with their effects? I could continue to look at my ego as the repository for all my bad traits, and battle it for my whole life. Or instead, I could transcend this common interpretation and talk about my ego's ability to *create impulse*. Now, I'm working with my ego constructively.

Ego creates impulse, and impulse is what drives us to *want things*. We want experiences. We want to consume life whether fast and hot or slow and easy. *How* we consume life is less important than the fact that the ego is often the propulsive mechanism that gets us to *want* to consume life. And by life, I don't just mean physical, material desires. Ego is what spurs our accomplishments. It makes us want to become a great piano player. Or to excel at tennis. Or to make the latest scientific breakthrough in your field. Or to get that capital for your new company. Or to get that woman to love you. Ego helps us complete the game we signed up for by helping us to acquire experiences, to help us begin to know ourselves, to help Source have the experience of Self. Ego fuels your pride, ambition, and need to perform to a higher standard—all impulses that help you gather more tasty experiences here, and incidentally which spur humanity as a whole toward greater accomplishments. Ego has helped propel us forward into the peak insights and breakthroughs of our greatest thinkers.

Stamping out the ego would be akin to a parent punishing a baby for crying; there can be no judgment on the actions of the ego. The ego is part of all of You—the Greater You—and it has a purpose in your life. It is the drive of Self, and *must* desire, crave, and want.

Remove ego and you remove impulse. Now, give yourself a break and start treating your ego as a friend. Revel in how it directs you to seek out new experiences and feel joy in recognizing how to use it constructively. Bring this poor child out of the dark corner of yourself. You'll be surprised at how it blooms into a positive partner in the light of your understanding and love.

Know Yourself to Manifest Yourself

Speaking of ego, if you talk to my family and the people I work with, they may tell you that I'm somewhat of an enigma. On the one hand, I'm sunny and optimistic, always suggesting that we have the power to mold our lives in any direction we choose. I'm generally thoughtful and grounded, and I have a good sense about the perils of becoming too full of oneself. In general, I have a lot of good points.

On the other hand, while I *am* extraordinarily humble regarding my importance to others, I have a pretty high opinion of myself, personally. I think I can do or accomplish just about anything, and I get impatient and frustrated when other people don't live up to the same expectations I hold for myself. And while I'm usually optimistic, I can occasionally be cynical, too. "He'll never change" is something that could easily come out of my mouth. So who am I, really?

As I go through my day, I'm aware of this mess of contradiction in myself. I see this same mess of contradictions in everyone I work with, from important media personalities to the guy who delivers the packages to our office.

And yet, our *lives*—not our contradictory personalities—are the ultimate showcases for who we really are. When we manifest, our lives are the result, so what we see around us is always the direct result of our real thinking, and our "real" personality.

My cynicism undoubtedly keeps me from experiencing some of the things that I would have loved to manifest by now. After all, our thoughts and feelings form the ceilings for what we can have. When I gripe about something, I'm adding validity to its existence—but a certain amount of pessimism is built into my personality. You see, as an expression of Source here for this life, I came in with some rules to make it interesting, many of which are the personality traits (whether genetic or nurtured in) that propel me.

We all contain a percentage of character traits that create boundaries for us, and our lack of understanding of these qualities puts a restraint on all we can have, be, and do. Some people are really smart, for example, but they have no common sense. Their constant bad decisions place barriers on their potential, and their lives express this. In other words, everyone has a grab bag of biologically based personality traits, physical attributes, and a basic level of intelligence that both contributes to their happiness and detracts from it. I work hard to know most of my own limitations—do you know yours?

WE THINK WE KNOW OURSELVES, but if we look at our lives right now and fail to see why we have what we do, then we're missing some important information about ourselves. We should be able to look at every part of our lives and understand how our thinking brought us here. In many cases, it's possible that we didn't actually create a situation, but we *allowed* it to form, almost by default. Even those situations that seem like something that's not part of us or that we didn't create, such as caring for a sick child or parent, are there by our will. We could have chosen not to care for that person, but we *did* choose to.

Your life—family, home, job, and health—is a mirror of your inner self. If you don't like what you see, figure out what part of you is responsible for creating this. Even if you blame certain conditions on the chaos of the unknown (such as with some health issues), you're still able to react or pre-act to alleviate the chaos and improve your situation.

What I'm getting at is that you're in a place of power once you realize what a gift it is to be able to use your life like a mirror for understanding. *Your external circumstances always reflect your internal grid.* Instead of feeling powerless or victimized (*I don't know why these awful things keep happening to me*), you can realize instead that your life never happens without you. The only time outside forces swoop in to wreck things is when you decide to put the blindfold on and drive through anyway, taking in whatever is in the road before you. This is when your default mode can either help you or hurt you. If you've Flowdreamed high standards, then even when you're not paying attention, you'll still stay in your Flow and in the path of good things.

When unprogrammed, or programmed with really awful parameters, your default mode lets your life fall to the lowest common denominator. You get the garbage heap of life and the end results of other people's situations.

Imagine walking into a virtual-reality game on the Internet. You enter the screen as your persona and see all kinds of people engaged in all kinds of dramas and activities. Now imagine these people coming over and asking you to participate because they need someone in their drama, and you never say no—you accept all offers, no matter how trivial, ugly, or demeaning. Before too long, you become a cog in another person's machine, simply fulfilling a role.

Well, that's just how many of us live, either predominantly or from time to time, *taking* what comes instead of *making* what comes. Even if we are more self-directed and work at defining the events we want to encounter, we'll still face unpredictable situations, trouble, and surprises . . . both good and bad. That is part of fulfilling our quest for self-knowledge and self-awareness—we want to know how we'll absorb and react to all kinds of interesting experiences. The difference is that as manifesters, we're always responding in ways that "course correct" and bring us back into that smooth, easy road where we get the most happiness.

Think about how you could work to manifest anything, such as poor health, personal drama, or any wretched circumstance, but you don't. Instead, you always want to realign yourself with the path that gives you what you want from life. You're waking up and realizing that you don't have to sleep through life—as you do, one thing you'll see more and more of is who you really are. Your life reflects this back to you every day. Don't be afraid of what you might see.

Making a Success of Any Situation

Because I tend toward impatience, it often comes out as annoyance—with my co-workers, my family members, friends, and even with politicians. It blows over, but I'm left wondering how this constant disgruntlement influences my ability to manifest. Frustration, as you can imagine, is an emotion that confirms the presence of a negative or irritating situation. In effect, it strengthens what you're putting an acknowledging awareness on. Just as with fear, brief frustration is a red flag that you're encountering something hostile to your happiness and Flow. It tells you, *Maybe you should take care of this,* or, *Warning: this isn't in your Flow.* But like fear, its positive impact can instead be rapidly turned toward creating *more* of the frustrating situation. This is why it's important to learn to make a success of every situation.

I'm reminded of a job I held years ago where I worked for a famous nutritionist, known worldwide and highly respected. I felt lucky to be a pupil of a man who'd helped revolutionize our understanding of natural health. As I quickly found, though, this man was "old school" in that he consistently disregarded the talents of his female workers. He didn't mean to be a chauvinist—it's just how he was raised, and he never had a reason to rethink it. Ironically, the women in his office doted on him and kept his organization running wonderfully. However, each time this doctor wanted to spearhead something new, he'd call in one of the many young male nutritionists or doctors who'd come to see him with their brilliant proposals. In every case, the young man was self-serving, and this older gentleman failed to see it time after time. I watched in horror as he was "taken" again and again.

Meanwhile, my frustration with my job mounted and mounted, until I dreaded everything from the drive to work to the endless hours spent in front of the photocopier doing mindless tasks, feeling like my talents were completely overlooked.

One day, I became so frustrated that I began writing a list of everything I was learning from my job. I wrote down things such as, "I'm learning that a person of any age or gender can have more value than what society would naturally give them," and "I'm learning that someday when I have employees, I'll always check in with them to see if they're feeling fulfilled or how I could better maximize their strong points or skills." I also wrote things that I discovered about myself: "I'm scared to ask for what I really want or say what I really think because I'm afraid that I'll be turned down or laughed at."

I kept adding to this list, until one day I realized that I didn't have to go to this job anymore. I hadn't merely outgrown the situation, but I'd actually made a success of it—if only to myself. I learned striking truths about the workplace and myself that may have taken me years to acquire otherwise. I also learned that I could create value in any situation, and that I didn't have to wait for someone else to recognize me or give me that value.

At the time, I called the job a "learning situation" (remember, I was still into suffering back then), but today I can see it in more neutral terms as a pattern of experience that was greatly enriching. The point is, when you make a success of your current situation, you turn the tide of energy surrounding you.

With practice, this ability to "turn the energy around" becomes reflexive. And to return to a topic that began this chapter, when you're able to make a success of any situation, you're getting to know yourself because you must first see your part in every encounter, then make smart choices toward your fulfillment in that encounter. Notice that I use "fulfillment" and "success" synonymously. Sometimes there won't be a traditional success, but since no one is grading you, what does it matter? Seek your fulfillment, whatever amount you can extract from your circumstances, then move on to another set of experiences. This is what the elusive term *success* really means.

Chapter 7

Relationships in the Flow

We talk so much about *things* when we discuss manifesting that you'd think it's only about materialistic gain. It's absolutely not. The material world is here for us to admire, experience, transform, and care for, but acquisition is not the pinnacle of our fulfillment. If anything, the attainment of objects becomes a poor substitute for the deeper, more intimate aspects of manifesting—such as the ability to form and express intimate relationships with others, whether family, friends, or lovers.

When discussing manifesting, it's often easier to use material objects and goals as examples, because it's easiest to identify the outcome of these requests. Also, you're interacting with inanimate things that don't have their own needs and desires.

But, at heart, manifesting is about *experience*—how you can create the experiences you wish to have in your life. It involves developing and getting to know yourself, becoming intimate with others, and increasing your knowledge of the world. What makes you happy? How do you share yourself with others? What do you, as an individual expression of God, mean to the world around you? This is what manifesting is really about.

Knowing yourself, offering yourself experiences, and participating in others' experiences are *life itself.* And lest you think this is extremely self-centered, consider that it's the sum total of your lifetime: You're born alone, process your emotions with no one else ever sharing your exact thoughts or feelings, and you move through death by yourself. You're an individual filament in the mind of God, perceiving, receiving, and giving alone. But you do all of this in tandem with everyone and everything else—separate but collectively.

The best way to get to know yourself in this journey is through collaboration with others. How will you know what really fills you up inside, if it weren't for the experience of love? How would you know just how much pleasure you could feel if it weren't for the collaboration of your children, who came into your life to experience you as their parent? Loving and interacting with one another is the most important form of creation and experience there is. We may be alone, but it takes sharing ourselves to truly indulge in life. It's a tango of opposites. If this weren't true, we'd each occupy our own planet, alone, in contact only with inanimate objects. How very boring for Source. What could It see or understand of Itself that way? And yet, by splintering Itself off into almost infinite pieces of perception (you and everyone else), It can see Itself reflected through countless eyes and from a multitude of perspectives.

Relationships are the driving force of our existence. Nothing material even comes close to the value of our intimacies with others. So why, then, do relationships cause such grief at times, and why do some of us seem to be on a track to create nothing but despair in our relationships, whether with family, co-workers, friends, or lovers?

As you know by now, we are each of a sliver of energy, a Flow of being, racing through this life experience. Like a bubbling brook, our Flow of energy is continually meeting other Flows (people, events, objects), which are like small streams running into our brook for a while before again splitting off into their own directions. We meet and merge with others' Flows, then disengage as we move into still other people's experiences and Flows. It's a continual cycle of merging and disengaging as our energy encounters others, completes the interaction, then moves away. Some meetings are brief—such as encountering the presence of the checker at the grocery store. The function of that meeting is known. Other encounters are prolonged, such as your relationship with your husband, wife, parents, siblings, or children. These interactions last a lifetime and the function is only vaguely defined, with each day offering new opportunities for interaction and continual redefining of the energetic encounter between you.

Manifesting for and with Others

In order to have a relationship of any kind—whether brief or extended, simple or complex—we must encounter the Source of another. And when we make this encounter, we bring in an agreement that, at face value, is as simple as, "We agree to have this encounter."

From there, the complexity of the engagement can soar. We bring expectations, needs, desires, and a slew of behaviors (ones we're aware of and ones we're not), and the other person does the same. We rely on words to communicate all of this, but words falter. Our deeper selves are likewise in connection with each other, offering a kind of energy handshake.

It's no wonder that every encounter has such potential to go in any direction. Given this, when you seek to manifest any type of relationship in your life, the most important factor to remember is that each individual is in control of his or her own experience, and no matter what you do, you cannot subvert, sway, or change another to meet your exact desires any more than someone else could do that to you.

I mention this because so often when people want to manifest within the area of their relationships, they become upset when the focus of their desire doesn't respond the way they want them to. They forget that every man or woman has total authority over his or her experience, and what you want and what another wants may or may not match.

One of the most common questions about manifesting for others is, "What can I do to help someone I love get through something in their life?" At best, you can create a Flow of energy potential for this person to encounter. This is another way of saying that you can call up the potential for situations to occur, but without the agreement (physically or energetically) of the other party, the desire won't move into play.

As an example, let's say that you're married and your husband has lost his job. He's in a funk and sliding into pessimism, despair, and depression; and you're both worried about paying your bills. You want to help him, but you worry that his pessimism will create resistance to whatever you try to bring in for him.

Your concern would be correct. You see, as he begins to project the strong emotions surrounding the feelings of *I won't get as good of a job as the one I had, No one is hiring in my industry,* or *I'm too old now for anyone to hire me,* he is indeed creating and attracting situations that will respond to his "requests" sent out through these emotionally charged thoughts.

When you step in and begin to feel his Flow bringing him wonderful opportunities as he happily accepts a terrific job offer, your energy is diverted by his stronger emotions, which modify his Flow. So to some degree, you're canceling each other out. However, if he should have hope and remain open, then no matter if he understands what you're doing or not, or even agrees with your philosophy, you'll still be able to help set up energy conditions that offer him better opportunities. But your husband *must* be open to seeing them and acting on them, because otherwise the force of his negative creation *will* bowl over the opportunities, never allowing them close enough for him to encounter.

You might bring in these opportunities by sensing the essence of your husband in his Flow (his energy signature, as opposed to seeing him physically), envisioning yourself next to him, and feeling you both riding forward in perfect alignment with your deepest Source selves. Once there, you'd begin to feel how desired he is in his field and how he begins to encounter fabulous luck in searching for a job, as just the right workplace is revealed to him and a wonderful connection is made. You'd picture your husband smiling with happiness as he tells you that he's accepted an offer, and you'd feel your emotions soaring with delight because he's again so joyous and fulfilled. Most of all, you'd focus on the emotional end points, "pre-acting" the feelings you anticipate for you both.

In this way, you're able to be a manifesting practitioner for another person. Some people are especially gifted at this. If it's something you wish to pursue, the best training is to develop the skills to manifest your own life first, then begin branching out with clearly defined desires for others—and make sure you have their agreement beforehand.

People are sometimes wary when you say that you're going to manifest something wonderful for them, much like the way you might feel if your mom says she's found you the perfect spouse, for instance. Your ideas of what to manifest and what another person desires may not match up.

For this reason, when manifesting on behalf of someone else, you should both clearly agree as to what you're creating *for* and *with* them. Your encounter with their Flow should amplify and solidify their own intentions.

When I hold my monthly Flowdreaming classes, this is exactly what I do. In these groups, I work with the energies of those involved to create a clear, shared imperative. Together, we program our Flows with our desires for all the best things in life. Our "programming power" is amplified by our collective intention. The effect is similar to a group meditation toward the same goal, or even to group prayer—one terrific reason for going to church. The difference, of course, is the nature of what we're doing: our goal is directed, intentional manifesting in the Flow.

Relationships as Flows of Communication

Let's look at another example of how relationships are really just Flows of interacting energy. A few weeks ago, a mother who was having trouble with her daughter called into my radio program. This woman's daughter would barely speak to her, and their relationship was having real problems. The mother was concerned about the girl's poor decisions, and she was worried that her daughter might be using drugs.

"What can I do?" the mother asked. "Can I help her without her even knowing it?"

"Yes," I replied. "It's possible to help her without telling her what you're doing. But you can't control what she will do to change, accept, or deflect what you're offering."

I told this woman to move into her own Flow by closing her eyes; opening to the feeling of a guided daydream; and sensing the fluid, forward feeling of her life in motion. Then I instructed her to bring to mind the feeling of her daughter—to bring up her appearance if she needed to, but most important, to bring up the essence of what her daughter feels like. Names and faces are transitory, but a person's energy signature is their soul, their Flow, their consciousness, and their collected experience that makes them who they are.

For instance, if you were looking for someone in what we call the "afterlife," or Heaven, would you stand there and envision a face and call a name: "John Smith! Where are you?" Not likely. Rather, you'd *feel* who he is, and send out that feeling as a *longing* for him. This is how you find someone in the Flow.

"Bring up your daughter's essence," I told my caller, "and offer her an invitation to Flow with you for a moment. Sense any response you get from this request. Do you feel hesitance? Curiosity?

"When you're contacting another person's Flow, remember that you're contacting something real; you're working with real energies and data on an energy level of thought that's outside of time and space, but nonetheless real. Oftentimes, even the most stubborn, hateful person isn't the same way within their deeper energy self. That self is often curious, open, and receptive—it's just been rejected and suppressed so often by the individual that when you contact it, it 'awakens' and is unusually open," I explained.

The daughter's Flow-essence was receptive to her mother, so I told them to Flow together. "Infuse your daughter with love," I instructed this mom. "Shower her with it, like you did when she was a baby in your arms, and let those feelings of love overwhelm you and make you cry. Sense this going into your daughter's energy, then send her a feeling that you want to talk to her, along with the assurance that you'll listen. Do *more* than tell her; *let her feel you listening.* Be aware of it inside yourself—a deep openness to whatever she has for you. Communicate emotion to emotion. Let words drop away.

"Continue to feel as if you're holding her, hugging her. Now experience absolute acceptance for whatever she reveals to you. Your daughter might tell you something now, in your Flow, as a message or feeling that you suddenly receive, or you could simply be defining a new emotional template for you both. You're creating an emotional sketch within the energies, and in essence saying, 'Okay, now manifest this into our physical lives. I have made the energetic counterpart to what I desire between my daughter and me. Now the physical circumstances will arrange themselves to create scenarios that can easily bring this interaction up and into play.'"

I told the woman to watch for opportunities and interactions in which this energy has the potential to easily pour through and not to be surprised if she finds herself replaying this exact scenario with her daughter in the real world in the future.

Finally, I said, "Make the potential situation stronger by going into your Flow and doing this every day—even a few times a day—each time reaching that peak state of loving openness and interaction with your daughter's Flow."

This woman is now realigning her Flow energy along with her daughter's, in the hopes that the girl will respond to this. Of course, her daughter could feel the energetic "tug" but stubbornly refuse the interaction in the physical world. She may sense an openness yet angrily reject the energetic request from her mother. But how many of us in the face of such repeated loving intention would ultimately resist such a peace offering?

You can use this same technique with anyone in the Flow—you could try it with your spouse or to heal an argument with a friend. You can ask for someone to call you or reach out to you. You can ask for someone to treat you better. You can ask for anything by calling up someone in the Flow and pre-acting the emotions of your desired relationship.

Making Someone Love You vs.
Allowing the Best Relationship

Can you ask for someone to fall in love with you? Yes, of course you could ask. But *should* you?

Some requests fall into a gray area. If you send overwhelming love and desire to another person and feel yourself being passionate with them, then even if they have no interest or are already committed elsewhere, you'll still impact them. This is no different than if you were to call someone on the phone and say, "Hey, let's get together. Let's have sex. Fall in love with me, okay?"

The difference is that you're being a bit more sly. So you may confuse the person, who feels bombarded by something they really don't want, but they can't tell you to bug off as easily as they could on the phone because the Flow has a ringer that doesn't stop. Do you really want to be that annoying caller who won't stop bothering someone?

Other people can always refuse you in their Flow. If you're chasing a woman who clearly has no interest in you, for instance, then she can simply shut you out of her Flow. But it's been my experience that people rarely do this, partly because they don't know they can. They're wide open, with no filters—their default mode is a home with windows and no screens. So tread carefully, obey the Golden Rule, offer other people choices, and don't manipulate their Flows into doing what you want.

If you try to force people to obey your will, you'll begin to feel unhappy and uncomfortable, because that is what your object of desire will be feeling in response to your manipulation. The Flow is a two-way connection, and you'll feel this other person's disturbed feelings fly back at you.

I don't know how else to say it except that your own Flow will tell you when to lay off.

And if you're truly following my advice, you're going to Flowdream for the most perfect, wonderful relationship ever, anyway—one that fulfills every longing in you and doesn't require you to persuade or cajole a specific person. You'll have left it to your Flow to find your perfect lover and set up the situations to bring you two together.

By focusing on just the one person you've already chosen to be "the one," you're very likely being that stubborn bird flying into a headwind and will probably experience continued obstructions and unhappiness in the relationship. All this argues in favor of simply setting up nice circumstances for yourself and others, ones that allow you to work out issues between you but don't force people into situations they don't want.

Disengaging Your Flow from Others

Speaking of situations we don't want, it's possible to Flowdream to rid ourselves of people or thoughts we don't want in our lives any longer. Years ago, for example, one of my family members was trying to get away from an old boyfriend who'd begun to stalk her. She and I worked together to cut off the Flow of energy between them so that he'd completely lose interest in her.

Do you remember how I said that all relationships move through a process of merging and disengaging Flows? Well, when you wish to leave someone, simply move into your own Flow and feel the essence of the other person disengaging from you. You'll have the feeling of a plug popping out of a wall socket or of the person drifting far,

far away from you. You'll sense the person swirling away behind you, out of your life and into the mists of time as you move forward in your Flow. If you create feelings of emptiness and nonconnection, the other person will lose all interest in you—and you in them—and you'll see their attraction and interest in you shriveling up until there's nothing left. In severing the ties in your energies, focus very lightly on the individuals themselves and heavily on preacting feelings of disinterest and disconnection.

You can also use this technique to sever your own obsessive thoughts about a former spouse or lover. With this technique in the Flow, it's possible to remove all the emotional energy you've built up that causes this person or obsessive situation to cling to you by simply feeling it all draining away behind you.

(Incidentally, this same technique can be used to soothe and release health issues—a topic I'm not focusing on too much in this book.)

There's so much I could say about working with the Flow involving other individuals. These ideas, though, give you an overview of some of the more popular themes I hear from men and women, and the Flow "recipes" I give them. Ultimately, what you find is that your Flow is more than just a place to manifest in. It's a soup of communication, wherein you can both send *and* receive information. Like the mother who was opening herself to receive communication from her daughter, you can open paths for energetic dialogue, since communication is the basis of all relationships.

Flowing with Like Energies

Have you ever thought about why groups of people cling together? On a basic level, we can say that human beings form tribes based on the will to survive—which we call "culture" or "society."

But on an individual level, we can often tell within moments of meeting people if our energies click. We take in their clothes, hair, face, body, scent, posture, expression, and more in just a few seconds. We have an immediate emotional reaction, before words are even exchanged. Sometimes our response is judgment—we make assumptions about them and have an emotional response to that (such as, *Oh she looks like a rich snob!*). But sometimes our response is more subtle, such as an unfathomable attraction, wariness, utter neutrality, or perhaps a curiosity to get to know the person better.

What *are* we really responding to? Is it purely physical?

Not at all. Each of us isn't just made from the physical bodies we inhabit, which we dress up and display to try to show others what kind of culture we want to be associated with (are we the suburban mom, the man at his white-collar job, or the hip young student with an artsy flair?). There are so many identities to choose from, and we migrate regularly through identities as we move in and out of new groups of friends and co-workers during the course of our lives. But beyond the external, there's also a more powerful attraction at work.

Imagine that each of us is a radiant body (but let go of your preconceived ideas about the "aura" for a moment) or a being of pure energy, and this energy is made from information. There is no physical component here—we're made of the coalescence of consciousness, pure data. So when we walk into a room full of other men and women, we're a body of information encountering all these other informational selves. What leaps out? Instantly, there's communication between all of us. This is why we can walk in a room and feel the "vibe" before even seeing who's inside.

Then, as we walk up to people, we encounter all their physical aspects (hair color, skin color, odor, pheromones, and so on), and this data is instantly received and processed simultaneously with another layer of information: this data-filled field of theirs. This nonphysical field stores all their feelings about themselves: their traumas, joys, opinions, and biases—as well as all their beliefs about themselves, from the superficial to the profound, such as "I'm ugly. I'm rich. I lie. I'm a good mother. I hate how I look in this dress today. I like this new hair color. I'm sensitive. I'm psychic. I'm emotionally damaged. I have a good heart. I have no one to love." Everything that this bit of Source, this person, has perceived is stored there.

Imagine if all these feelings you have about yourself—and the results of all the experiences you've had—were being broadcast on a lit billboard hung around your neck. You might be appalled at what this board was saying to the world, but at least we'd all be on equal footing because we all both send and receive this data.

In only seconds, we combine all the physical and energetic information we receive about another person, and that becomes his or her "vibe." And we can tell in that same instant whether or not we'll get along or repel each other, like two magnets.

Think about if you've ever had a truly bizarre attraction to someone. You may have said to yourself, "This guy isn't even my type—I don't like his body, and I hate his attitude—but there's just something about him that inter-ests me. What's going on?"

Remember that this person contains so much more than the surface information you're receiving from his physical self. He's probably had many experiences like your own—feelings, thoughts, and encounters all piling up into streaks of similarity to you that your deeper self instantly recognizes and identifies with. Surfaces can be vastly dif-ferent, while interiors can be remarkably the same.

This same phenomenon holds when you meet someone you *think* you should like. Maybe you meet an individual who seems like she could be a good friend: she shares your love for spirituality, hula dancing, and motorcycles. Except there's that one thing you just can't stand about her, and you use this apparent flaw as a good rationale for why you dislike her so much. It's impossible for you to see past this quality of hers and it irritates every part of you. However, despite what you think, it's not this behavior of hers that really gets to you—it's something much more fundamental.

Again, surfaces can be deceiving, since looking at them is like looking at the top of a pond. You have no idea how deep the pond is without going under the surface. Perhaps this person who "rubs you wrong" is so dissimilar to your core energy field that it's akin to mixing oil and water—some energies just don't interact well. You've probably also encountered people to whom you felt an instant revulsion or distrust . . . they just felt *creepy.* Something about their energy signature was repugnant to your own.

And then, there are the truly foreign. I've had three or four encounters in my entire life with people who struck me as immediately uncategorizable—*alien.* Now, I'm not saying that these people *were* aliens, but their energy fields were so foreign as to create a response in me of unease, confusion, and intrigue. I almost felt "displaced" as I interacted with them.

I can only speculate what kind of information these people's fields contained, but what they were "telling" me with their data-filled selves was so far outside my experience as to be unrecognizable—as if I were looking at Egyptian hieroglyphics and trying to read the markings. Wherever the energy beings in their bodies came from, the bulk of their accumulated experiences were so far removed from my own that we seemed to be speaking different languages to each other.

Randomness, Intention, and Chaos

A few years ago, as my mother was rounding a mountain bend in her car, a man on a motorcycle in the opposite lane lost control and slid across the road at 60 miles per hour into the side of her car. On the other side of her was a drop-off hundreds of feet to the ground, but luckily the car spun away from the cliff. She was unhurt, but the motorcyclist was injured. Injured, but not dead—not free-falling off the cliff to the ground below. Her car, there at that particular moment, was the only thing that kept this man from sliding over the cliff to his death.

Since the accident, we've often wondered why this happened. Why did he lose control at that precise moment so that their two unrelated Flows could intersect? Why did he live? Had my mother volunteered, in some other energy plane, to be part of this encounter?

From a larger perspective, she and this man both live in a common area. Since each of them drives and takes this road frequently, they each also assume certain risks as part of their Flow by living near this mountain road and driving on it. But still, why did these risks materialize so spectacularly, and why then? Was this *random?*

Randomness represents uncertainty in the Flow. Every natural object has a quotient of randomness within it—of chaos or instability. It's as if this penchant for chance was built into the fabric of our reality, as if Source said, "Let's not make things too ordered or predictable. Let's let things get mixed up from time to time, and see what happens. I'll bet that some disorder, some *chaos,* will continue the creative expansion of time, space, and experience in more interesting and novel ways."

Think of the random events that infuse life, from the smallest events to the largest. In every dividing cell, for instance, mutations occur that lead to opportunities to either evolve or die, as a result of random chance. The cell isn't necessarily choosing its evolution, it's buffered by the element of uncertainty.

Uncertainty exists everywhere. In a storm system, temperature, humidity, and precipitation mix to create volatile, explosive weather patterns. Each raindrop falls on a random path, and each bolt of lightning strikes the earth in unpredictable places.

Part of the fun in our adventure is that there are so many unknown elements that become part of the experience. Think of it as a "rule" in this game—we can plan, but in this poker game we call life, we may not know the next card drawn. Similarly, an artist doesn't know exactly how the paint will fall from her brush, even with the most careful and steady hand and the greatest intention for how the piece will turn out.

We always work in a combination of intention and randomness. For many of you reading this, these words are chilling because they set a limit on our power to "make" things happen. Instead, we must realize that we're more in the business of "suggesting" that things happen—of *coaxing* them into being or setting up sympathetic energy conditions to *allow* them to happen. A knitter makes the stitch and has a vision for the garment, but she doesn't know exactly how that stitch will look until it's completed. Will her fingers slip and drop the stitch? Will the yarn twist?

Action creates potential; potential creates the opportunity for randomness. Your pre-action of an emotion intended to attract a matching situation will set forth an energy condition, but the exact situation you'll encounter is still based on myriad potentials coming together—some random, some planned, but still pressed into the focused "laser" quality of your intention, much as a laser focuses light. Your desire focuses outcomes, but the light contained in this laser is full of random events coming together into a cohesive whole. The dance of chaos and intention is ongoing.

There's great power in acknowledging that both intention and chaos are always in play. For example, you may have *allowed* in sickness without purposefully *intending* it. You may have been moving through your life like a blindfolded driver behind the wheel of your car, careening toward your future, crashing into whatever chaotic experiences came before you—these included sickness, pain, accidents, or what have you. But by recognizing your responsibility for the conditions around you, and taking the blindfold off as you realize your potential for manifesting, you simultaneously assume the ability to alleviate or remove all the illness or unhappiness you've previously allowed in.

However, you still must temper this awareness with an understanding that you're limited within this game of life. You may be *of* God—a sliver of perception gathering within It vast amounts of self-awareness—but you've to come this place with a limited set of tools. You weren't given the tools for certain intentions—such as to grow wings and fly. You signed up for a game with rules, and one of these rules is the unexpected. God does not always want to know what's just around the corner. Where's the self-exploration if the unknown is already known? Sometimes God plays peeka-boo with Itself. So do you.

Part II

Flowthinking

"Experience isn't interesting till it begins to repeat itself—in fact, till it does that, it hardly is experience."

— **Elizabeth Bowen,** Irish author

We're now moving into deeper waters. You've seen what Flowdreaming is and learned how to do it, so now let's put it in a larger context as I share some of the revelations that working with the Flow has led me to over the years. Together, these musings and revelations form what I loosely refer to as "Flowthinking"—the background understanding of what the Flow actually is.

Chapter 8

The Nature of Source

Let's look at our feelings about who we are, what we are made of, and our relation to the most creative energy in our universe. Understanding this opens the door to Flowthinking, and provides you with a deeper understanding of the energies you're working with.

It all begins with our connection to God, or Source. Religions have given us many reasons for why humanity supposedly left God. You're of course familiar with the classic Western allegory of Adam and Eve: humans were created, we sinned, and we were punished; and we've been seeking our Father's forgiveness ever since. Once we accept God again through His son, we'll be welcomed back home.

Other major religions throughout the world have similar creation stories and means for worshippers to be brought back into God's Kingdom. Usually they involve us having to "shape up" somehow and follow the Creator's somewhat vague, capricious, or difficult directions. For example, another explanation is that we'll only return to God (pure bliss, love) when we reach a state of enlightenment found through spiritual discipline, purification, and/or revelation through having had multiple past lives or learning experiences as we eliminate karmic debt.

And in the burgeoning world of alternative spirituality, there are even more theories and so-called truths swirling around that account for our supposed separation from God. One in particular describes life as "nothing but a dream." In this dream, we separated from our Creator because we wanted to experience the act of creation ourselves and had to "leave" Him in order to do this—the only way being through the illusion of a dream. But now that we've become lost in this dream, we desperately want to wake up again.

At the heart of all religions is the idea that separation from God—in one form or another—results in suffering, and unity with God results in love and pleasurable feelings. You can subscribe to any story line you want regarding the question of why we're supposedly separate from God or why we suffer, because ultimately (and despite what any group says), no one knows with 100 percent certainty.

What's more, the love we feel for each other and the intimacy we develop when experiencing God's creation on Earth are mere shadows of true divine love, and it's generally agreed that all we encounter here in physical form is a poor substitute for the realm of unadulterated Source. So not only are we stuck here in life, but we've been put up in the equivalent of a second-rate motel. God created a playground for us that was inferior to the rest of Its vast vacation spots.

I offer you another perspective. In this one, God is a great engineer and an artist. Source thinks, *I wish to explore the many facets of all that I encompass. To do so, I will need self-awareness. Self-awareness means that I will have to have perspective. Perspective means the ability to look as if from the outside in. So, I must create a sensation of separation so that I may enjoy this self-awareness and this coming to know who I am. I cannot see myself if I do not create something of myself to look at me.*

As the desire for self-awareness is launched, a multitude of creative ways to achieve this come into being: humans, aliens, ecologies, galaxies, energy intelligences of unknown names, and more—all with the purpose of creating a vision for God of Itself. Imagine a room suddenly filled with trillions of filaments of light, filling every molecule of space in that room. As each filament occupies its own small space, it absorbs and *knows* that space. Like God turning Itself inside out to see what's inside, we are God's perception of self—the *eyes* of God.

Sometimes I envision Source energy as a beautiful fabric—a white, sparkling material that floats in the unseen breeze of life. Except when you look closer at this fabric, you see that it's taken up by an almost infinite number of bright eyes—every inch is filled with an eye, each looking upon the other. As this fabric becomes scrunched or folded, all eyes are now only looking at one another, so God looks around and only sees Itself. This sheet of shining consciousness, of eyes, has no end to it and is everything—animal, vegetable, and mineral. From burning suns to tiny slivers of grass, each contains the capacity to offer God a tiny insight into Itself. Some eyes are bigger and hold greater depths of awareness, and others are almost blinded.

Each eye is actually a pinprick of consciousness, a lens through which God sees; and these lenses, or eyes, offer God a unique vision of Itself colored by the perceptions and experiences unique to that lens. That's what God is: self-awareness, made from all the self-awareness that we collectively are.

In this scenario, the separation between us and God isn't fueled by our guilt or because we've been shut out of the kingdom. The separation is joyful! What's more, there's only a *perception* of separation, which is intentional, voluntary, and immediately reversible should Source, or any part of It, choose. There is no separation at all, really. It's only a splitting of perception: there's the one doing the seeing and the one being seen. God looking at Itself. You looking at yourself.

Further, nothing God makes is inferior, or better or worse than, anything else across the playground of Self. It's all made of the same energy. Heaven and Earth stand in equal favor in God's eyes—only the experiences to be had in each are different.

To make the game more interesting, and to make the exploration more appealing, God has chosen to make Its "filaments of awareness" exist within different environments. Within each environment are a set of "rules of reality" that massage the perception of the inhabitants toward different focuses—or contrasting lenses of sight. These lenses create belief systems, attitudes, and cultures; and these rules create distinctive fields of difficulty. There are rules that produce suffering while others facilitate joy, just like some "eyes of God" are playing Mother Goose while others are playing a high-stakes game of life and death. God wants it all, just as humans go for the romantic comedy *and* the blood-and-guts thriller when going to the movies.

Remember, God isn't judging Itself in "how well It plays." Source is *reveling in the experience of playing.* Because there's so much suffering here doesn't mean that there's much of it *everywhere* in this Universe, or in any other layers of energy containing intelligences that may be out there. But here, hardship is part of the construct, and it forces us into new emotional insights and dilemmas. It adds to God's awareness of all that It is. God doesn't "approve" of suffering, killing, and terrorizing; It simply has no judgment about it. There is a difference.

If God wanted to stop suffering, It could. We don't need to wait for a "higher" energy to step in and do it for us. *We* are of God, and if we made the collective choice to obliterate most forms of sorrow (as caused by famine, war, disease, violence, and so on), we could easily do this as a society. We have all that's required: leadership, will, scientific insights, creativity, and physical bounty. So misery, in many instances, is a matter of *choice.* Right now, we *choose* to allow people to suffer. It's possible to remake society along a set of guiding principles that honor life, individual and collective integrity, long-term sustainability, and the spirits of individuals to have every option when defining their destinies (as opposed to society today, which primarily honors power, wealth, and consumption).

So God is a vast field of energy engaged in a continual act of self-expression and increasing awareness. And everything is made from God—everything *is* God. Source uses no materials other than Itself to create from. Therefore, conscious awareness is threaded through the Universe, through everything in existence, to greater and lesser degrees. You, in your body, occupy a vessel that contains a quantity of awareness. A tree also contains some degree of perception. A rock, while containing even less, is still occupying a Flow of its own energy or godliness, because it too will change form and collect experience as time and its environment break it down into a new form of energy. All this is known, and experienced, by God.

Such interconnected awareness means that all bits of matter are in play, infused with the ability to change and move. Doesn't this sound curiously like Flow energy? You're right—it *is* Flow energy. Flow is God. Flow is Source. Flow is the fundamental stuff of creation—the flowing perception of God experiencing Itself.

Your Flow is a progression of one small particular flowing thread of awareness within a matrix of uncountable other threads. God is an ocean of being, and each of us is a water molecule dancing in this ocean, distinct and separate, but part of the whole as well. This is the wellspring of creation and manifesting, and of unheralded potential that we've barely developed a sense of.

Chapter 9

The Greater You

So, you might think, *who am I within this creation scenario?* I'm sure you can tell by now that this idea of manifesting, or Flowdreaming, does take a few metaphysical truths for granted. One is that this essence called the Flow exists, and that it encompasses all known and unknown matter as well as vibratory realms of conscious awareness we can't easily describe or even know. Collectively, Flow in its largest sense is the mind or self-perception of God Itself. In its smallest sense, it can be the trajectory of a bee buzzing around a flower, a single human thought, or an organic molecule. It's *all* God, all currents of energy in various forms and degrees of interconnectedness. Flow spans all of life—a great ocean with its many subcurrents—and understanding this is the essence of Flowthinking.

Within this great sea of all that is, you exist not merely as a physical component collecting data or experience through this process called life, but you extend deep within it to whatever ultimate expansiveness there is—what you may call God, Source, universal awareness, or the Great Spirit. Gaining this expanded view of yourself is crucial to understanding how easily the Flow works on your behalf, and it also helps answer that question of how you know what's in your Flow (and what isn't).

Let's review your place with the energies: Imagine yourself like a sparkling string extending the length of a vibratory scale. At the deepest "depth," you're a pure component of Source, one of God's infinite eyes of perception. At the other end of that string is the material component of yourself that's participating in a material existence under the imposition of time, space, and uncertainty—locked in a game intended to yield to you revelations of insight and experiences. This is Source experiencing Itself in "slow time," in increments of each moment as a human here. In this physical end point of the "dancing string of you," you're constricted by your surroundings—namely our four dimensions. Your perception is limited to this area of your exploration.

Since your current perception is physical, it makes sense that you mainly experience your physical vibration—that is, your body. You're largely closed off from the other aspects of your Self because your physical self is where your point of awareness is located . . . for now.

Now think of your *mind* as merely a deeper or finer gradation of energy. Like your body, it stores vast quantities of data, but carried in a different medium—one that we don't readily perceive. Your mind is a bridging mechanism that allows the physical you to access the deeper levels of Self, similar to a conduit. Your consciousness extends beyond the neurons of your brain, since your true mind isn't in your brain—it's more of a field of awareness that extends beyond your physical self. This mind field encompasses all your thoughts and self-perceptions, and all that "thinking" you do is more like the result of your brain processing your mind's thoughts, originating some material, but not all.

Beyond this "mind strata" are still more degrees of the energy being that is you. We've named this the soul, but it isn't some ghostly aura; it's merely one more level of information, and the "place" it inhabits is right here with you now, hidden within the layers of energy it exists through. The soul isn't some separate, discrete thing—it's just a name that's applied to a whole swath of your Self that exists in ways you have trouble perceiving from this physical perspective. Like looking through a frosted glass window, you're unable to see what's truly there.

Your sense of self, of "youness," is what's lovingly called your soul. But even "soul" is a misnomer, for it sounds like another "part"—something that could be lost or stolen or separated from you. In reality, it's no more separate than any certain length in the string of you could be separate from that string. It's always part of you, but existing in a depth of energy you can't easily perceive.

In fact, we could extend this and say that there are even greater depths to us than our souls. While the soul is the repository for the experiences we collect as an "eye of God," there's even more information beyond that for us to understand. Past the soul, it's only a guess as to how deep our Selves exist. I find it easy to believe that our sense of self permeates reality to the degree that Source is the collected perceptions of all of us and everything else, meaning that who we are is actually without end—in other words, there's no "final boundary" to ourselves.

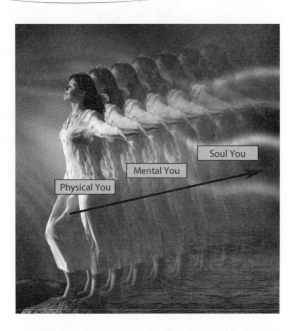

You exist at all times along a continuum of energy, along with everything else in the world. Your body is just the very edge of the Greater You, like the skin of an orange. Instead of seeing your body, mind, and soul as three separate and distinct things, think of them as gradations of energy along a vast spectrum, existing simultaneously along this continuum of energy—the Flow.

These "yous" exist on finer and finer levels, from the outside, visible You (your body) to the inner, invisible You (your mind and spirit). Your consciousness is a bridge between these levels. During your day, your consciousness is both present in your brain and at the same time receives a huge amount of information from the part of itself that exists in the Flow—in other words, in these finer vibratory frequencies.

When you purposely move into the Flow, you're moving into and aligning yourself more firmly within life's finer energy fields, where reality takes shape at its most basic level. Every time you think, you're moving in and out of these finer fields at a quantum level. Flowdreaming allows you to expand your access to these finer fields, where the world as we know is first thought into reality.

Who Is This Greater You?

Redefining the mind and soul challenges you to rethink many beliefs you may have accumulated. For instance, you're never in danger of losing your soul because it isn't separate and cannot be taken or harmed. It simply *is*— existing as a wash of energy containing vast amounts of data in levels of reality that we barely understand. It's not attached with a silver cord and can't roam the earth as a ghost. Neither is it not an object to be bartered, any more than you could peel the skin off your own body.

Your soul acquires the kind of energy that you experience. If you experience tragedy and misery, you offer that to your deeper energy self to carry as part of its experience. If you experience joy and lightness of being, your soul becomes imbued with that, and it radiates from you like a shining light. If your soul has accumulated deep quantities of anger, then the anger becomes you—this could be a rationale for what we think of as karma, when in reality we're simply creating more of what we are.

The only judgments the soul experiences are the observations that come from others. For instance, I may meet you and feel the weight of your soul and think, *What sadness she has inside her.* But God doesn't judge you. God, or Source, may feel impelled to collect some kinds of experiences over others (a feeling of desire is different than judgment), but God has no end game in mind for what It is—whatever we add to It is what It is.

Collectively, I call this expanded you the "Greater You." I purposely use the term *Greater You* instead of the more popular *Higher Self* because I want to detach you from any old associations you may already have to the term Higher Self so that you can think about yourself from a fresh perspective. I also dislike the implication that "higher" somehow means better, smarter, or more evolved; like a parent looking down in judgment on their dumber child self. Move away from such judgments. Think in terms of expansion, depths of perception, and horizontal movement, and less in terms of higher/lower, good/bad, and accomplishment/defeat.

At times, you'll find yourself moving between different levels of your Self, or Greater You. Like a bead bouncing on a vibrating string, your point of awareness is at times solely body based, but at other times as the bead swivels and slides, running the length of the string, your awareness can originate from the deeper self. We've all had those experiences in which we felt an attunement, a deep profundity, in which the "light" suddenly shines on our awareness. For instance, as I've written certain passages in this book, I've been consumed with bliss—a feeling of awe and rapture at having touched a fundamental truth, which has washed over me like a lover's fingertips. I have accessed this deeper self, and felt its vibration as a kind of ecstasy.

When you Flow, you purposefully and consciously move your awareness into these deeper parts of self and become tuned in to your Greater You. It's a great tragedy that so many people feel cut off from the rest of themselves, but then again, this tragedy is part of the experience as well . . . some choose to sleep, while others are more awake.

The Greater, Expanded You is always with you. When you have an experience, It has it, too. When you cry, It feels sadness; when you're pleased, It feels pleasure. Therefore, when you offer a desire or request to your Flow, your Greater You also reinforces this desire in keeping with the deeper energies of Itself. However, this Greater You taps resources that seem hidden—when you ask for something, as the old saying goes, the Universe will deliver.

While the Universe certainly does respond, your Greater You figures out how this response will be orchestrated and revealed to you. Your Greater You has a perspective you can't hope to have in this limited world. If you ask for something you really want, feel its presence in your Flow, program in this desire, and challenge the Flows of everything outside of you to match your desire; your Greater You is able to orchestrate the means by which this desire best fits into your life.

Think of a busy intersection where the traffic lights have stopped working and cars are charging through. This is the busy crossroads of Flow in motion, except there are more than four lanes—there are millions. If you, in your small perspective, were to step into the middle of this intersection to try to guide the traffic, you'd be overwhelmed and unable to see around the hundreds of thousands of cars that immediately surrounded you.

Your Greater You is a much more effective traffic cop; after all, it lives in these energies. It's at home here, so manifesting your desires is as simple for your Greater You as navigating a two-lane road is for you. Wouldn't you expect your Greater You to help out?

Sometimes the idea of your deeper self as actively engaged in helping you define your future set of experiences is a revelation. Either you've believed in a Higher Self that passively directs you but is fairly out of reach, or you've believed only in a soul that never really becomes engaged in life and is merely a passive recipient for certain amounts of good or evil you've tucked into it via your thoughts and actions. It's time to think of your soul/Higher Self/Greater You as an ally—as engaged in helping you squeeze the juice from your life as you are. We often ask for help from guides, helpers, or angels, but ultimately, there's no one who knows you better, loves you more, or understands exactly what you need to make you happy other than yourself.

Another way of looking at it is that you, in physical form, are like a person standing with your nose against a brick wall. Your perception is of the tiny cracks, flakes of rock, and mortar right before your eyes. While you are indeed seeing the brick wall, your perspective limits you to seeing only one tiny portion of it. Your Greater You, however, has a much wider perspective. From its vantage point, it sees the whole wall, as well as over, around, and below it, too. Engaging your Greater You to work with you allows a huge increase in opportunities to flow through to you. Whenever you're faced with a seemingly insurmountable problem, your Greater You has a broader view that most likely includes not just one solution, but many.

Keep in mind that the concept of Flow presumes that life happens on many levels, not just the physical one you see around you. It makes sense that *you* also happen on many levels. If the Flow is multilayered, and you're part of the Flow, then you're multilayered, too. Incredible potential exists in this Greater You, and it's always present and working on your behalf as the orchestrating part of your deeper vibratory scale. It's a container for organizing and preserving your past experience, a filter for understanding the meaning of it, and a guide for acquiring more of the experiences you want. Imagine yourself—all of your thoughts, feelings, and self-awareness—and now imagine that something else has been added that's a whole new dimension, filled with senses and perceptions you can't even dream of. You only know that you're expanded in the most glorious sense. Not only are you expanded, but you're loved, preserved, and protected as if by the most loving parent you can imagine. All of this is the Greater You.

We always want something outside ourselves to take care of us—whether it's angels, guides, dead relatives, spirits, or even God—because fundamentally, we don't trust ourselves to do it. If you find yourself more willing to trust an angel or spirit guide than the deepest, wisest, more-in-touch-with-Source aspect of yourself, then ask yourself why.

We're not talking about the small, limited you—the one who's locked into a tiny perspective in life, makes poor decisions, doesn't know which way to go, and has allowed itself to be hurt over and over. We're talking about the glorious You who extends through all the energies of the world—directly part of Source Itself—that's flavored with your unique perspective containing all the experiences you've ever taken in. The part of You that orchestrates, catalogs, and narrates all your existence, working in tandem with (neither higher nor lower than) all the other energies of God out there. *Remember, if you always look for love or wisdom outside yourself, you'll never meet the God within yourself.*

When you go into your Flow, open your senses to your Greater You. Listen for thoughts that drop into your mind. Be aware of feelings or impulses that wash over you, and be on the lookout for communication through pictures or memories that surface while there. Your Greater You is delighted to communicate with you whenever it can, however it can.

Ask your Greater You to help you achieve your desires. Ask that it open the best possible routes for you, and that it find the easiest, most reliable, and most honorable means for getting what you want out of life. Don't just offer your request to your Flow—offer it to all of You that exists within your Flow. Your Greater You delights in organizing experiences for you.

Chapter 10

Patterns, Paths, and Life Purpose

Let's think again about the design of your life. Now, you probably have some expectations about how it will all work out—not hopes, but *expectations*. Hopes are what you really wish would happen—what you want yet feel isn't possible for one reason or another. Expectations are what you think is doable, feasible, practical, and most likely to happen.

Right now would be a good time to try an exercise using pen and paper. Draw two columns on the paper and title them "Hopes" and "Expectations." Under "Hopes," jot down all those things you wish you had in your life or how you want to be living it; in the other column, write just how close to those hopes you think you can realistically get.

You'll probably see a huge difference between the two. For example, your "Hopes" column might include having a vacation home, unlimited income with little effort required to maintain it, and the pleasure of a large and loving family. However, your "Expectations" column could include comments such as, "I'll never get a vacation home, but it would be nice to pay off the home I have," "I'll never get an unlimited income, but it would be nice to get a job I actually enjoy," and "Maybe I'll have a huge family, but right now I'll settle for having a good romance."

When we hope, we're suggesting a template for our dreams in the way an artist visualizes the canvas before he sets his paintbrush to it. Now, any artist can tell you that the execution of this image—what's actually created—is always different than what's in his mind's eye. But the initial vision flavors or characterizes the reality. The "hopes," or the ideals that you have, likewise show you the *overall direction and tendency* for your truest inner happiness. You don't need to believe that you must manifest every detail of your dreams, just as the artist knows that the painting will be beautiful and satisfying in its own unique way, though always different from his original idea.

Your hopes tell you the landscape you'd be happiest within. They point the way to the direction of your next *patterns of experience.*

Patterns vs. Ladders

Patterns of experience is a phrase I use a lot. It helps me think of my life as a series of new and interesting encounters, rather than as a road full of life lessons or a path that I can stray from. It also reminds me that every step can branch out in any direction. This is what unnerves some people who want a *path* to follow. But those who manifest understand the true power in being able to step in any new direction at any time. I know that following the course of my hopes toward a landscape I'll be happiest in means that I must have the ability to swivel in any direction I choose. And this landscape may continually be changing, growing, or moving into new areas.

This is an important point: we often think that there's some particular direction we *must* go in—that there's some perfect life or set of goals meant for us to achieve—and that it's all about figuring out, or being shown, what that is. We wait for someone to tell us what we're meant to do that will make us completely happy; otherwise, we get frustrated as we try to discover what we "came here to do." Then we judge ourselves on how well we are or are not fulfilling this supposed mission.

On top of that, we create a list of things we think we must do in order to be happy in whatever particular order we've put together for ourselves: become a parent, homeowner, top employee, successful entrepreneur, and so on. Often, there are items on this list that we're barely consciously aware of, but that nevertheless drive us. These are our hidden expectations, which were instilled in us somewhere along our journey and not ones we decided on ourselves. Further, each of these expectations is an opportunity to judge ourselves and the character flaws that prevent us from achieving these goals or getting them just right.

WHEN I LOOK AT MY LIFE, instead of seeing a series of goals to accomplish or a life purpose to fulfill, I instead envision a rich and luxurious quilt, bespeckled with many interesting colors and patterns. Each square represents time I've spent in a particular set of experiences in my life. No part of the quilt is more revered than any other, and there's no particular direction I must go in next. My "life purpose" will be revealed to me when I hang up my completed quilt at the *end* of the road, at which point I'll see the majesty of what I've created. What a relief to know this; I don't have to find a perfect path *now* with my quilt of life far from complete.

I recognize that my time in this body is about exploring all the situations and opportunities that come my way. No one way is more "correct" than another. All experiences have their interesting qualities. And I further know that I won't just take what comes, blundering blindly about and taking what is shoved at me, piecing a haphazard crazy quilt, but I'm actively cultivating those kinds of interesting experiences that I want to have. I'm engaged in a daily manifesting of the upcoming circumstances. This is what it means to live within my Flow and become adept at the art of manifesting through Flowdreaming.

So, if my *hope* is to have a free, easy lifestyle, then I use Flowdreaming to draw this into being. Because of the nature of the Flow philosophy and practice, my *expectation* is that my desires will be delivered to me, and I become curious to see just *how* my hopes will be fulfilled and what kinds of experiences will begin to fill up my time. In this way, I grow more closely aligned with myself: my hopes and expectations work in tandem with each other, alongside that seemingly magical quality of manifesting to present an ever-changing array of experiences to fill me up. The disconnect between hopes and expectations becomes much less, although my wishes still act as the suggested course or route rather than an absolute path. Most important, I'm not *climbing* toward anything in particular; rather, I'm *exploring*.

By letting go of the "ladder" perception of living, I also allow myself the chance to go in new directions more easily, instead of feeling the constant pressure to move upward or toward some profound unknown destiny. I know that when I make changes that might appear dumb or backward to some people, I'm really just in a transitional phase and may not be stepping down a rung at all—I'm just looking into a new place for a while to see what's there.

If you can identify with, and put into practice, what I'm hammering away at—that you can get off the treadmill mentality that permeates our society—you'll go a long way in becoming more satisfied with what you're manifesting.

"You Ain't Here to Learn Lessons"

Another fallacy we tend to believe is that we're here to learn lessons and/or go through certain, preordained life experiences.

Over the years, I've had many long discussions with people about this concept. What I see is that many people in the metaphysical field have come up with an alternate rationale for the age-old question of why we suffer. While a Christian may say that we go through hardships because it's God's will—or because we're punished for our sins—and that we're being judged by how well we fulfill God's laws, a person of metaphysical or more Eastern thinking would say that it's because we've chosen a learning experience (something dreadful or anguishing that's meant to toughen us up to bring us one step closer to enlightenment).

Either way, we just can't seem to get away from the basic explanation that we're here to get through a series of difficulties in order to learn through pain. Once again, a belief that we need lessons based on punishment or reward is the antithesis of manifesting, since it gives our power away to some other force or system.

Yes, we do choose experiences that cause us to grow. The distinction is the rest of the idea: some believe that these learning experiences are here to somehow purify us and make us become an older, wiser, or even more enlightened soul—maybe a soul on its so-called last life. In other words, we're again pressed to a ladder in which we have to complete a series of exercises, be judged by how well we accomplish them, and then maybe be rewarded—like a kid who's told that she has to master the material or risk flunking, or a person who's in danger of going to hell or never reaching nirvana if he doesn't tow the line and "get with God's program." Doesn't "learning lessons" sound a lot like some of our other popular religions—just with a slightly different dressing?

Here's a thought: what if we've *already* been enlightened, reached nirvana, merged with God's love, been forgiven for any "sin" we may have committed, and lived in heaven? What if the part of us here inhabiting these bodies just wants to get to know Itself more, so It came here to have experiences? It knows It will do both good and bad things and feel both joy and suffering. It just wants the experiences to reveal to Itself who It is as It encounters situations and thrusts back responses to them. We may indeed choose learning experiences in order to enrich ourselves, but we may also decide to enter certain situations because we're curious for the adventure as a means to get to know ourselves.

I suggest this idea to get you to break out of what might be your current tendency toward linear thinking and to get you off the strict, straight-ahead path of continual self-improvement. *What if there's nothing to improve upon?*

"Well," you may argue, "This smacks of heresy. What is the point of that? Where's the *goal* there? I can certainly think of some people who could use improvement!"

Again, as you consider this idea that you have lessons to learn or sins to avoid, think about the description of Source energy I gave you. Then, ask yourself why God would seek to purify or "teach" Itself things, then grade Itself through coming here in physical form to slog through trials. I'm talking about *you* here. You are made from God's own materials. You are a part of Source energy. God did not find the materials to make you by using anything outside Itself. God did not make an inferior product or a flawed thing that needs improving. If God gave you self-determination and free will, then God knew what It was doing. Your nasty habits and impure thoughts are as much of God's creation as your generosity and empathy. Source *is* perfection. Whether you call it God, Source, consciousness, universal awareness or whatever other name you choose, the heart of this idea is that we are all a piece of God, experiencing this creation we are all making together. God does not need to judge Itself. God observes, God enjoys, God suffers, but it does not grade itself. And you are made, truly, in God's own likeness, because you are part of God.

Each of us, in our act of perceiving our lives as we move through them, is like a video camera funneling information back into Source. As God's eyes, we revel in experiences that constantly fill Source up with almost unlimited amounts of information about Itself. Through you, Source gets to see and experience Itself. How glorious is that! *God gets to know Itself through you.* What an important job you have!

Why would this magnificence choose to see Itself as somehow "less than" or needing to improve? It grows in understanding just through observing all the minutiae of Its creation, including you. If you choose to have an awful experience that you justify as a "lesson I have to learn," God smiles at that as easily as It smiles on the other person who has a harmonious, loving experience. Both are interesting, and both offer glimpses into Itself.

Take a minute to explore this thought, and reread this section of the book if you need to.

WHEN IT COMES TO LESSONS, you need to plan them. Lessons imply an agenda and forethought as you set up the desired end point, and the challenge to help you achieve that. Theoretically, you could either set up these challenges or lessons before your birth, or in the potent "now." If you're locked into thinking of time as linear, always believing that you planned a series of life lessons before birth, then you're making a bet that the lesson will still be relevant by the time you get to it. It would be like setting up a sixth-grade test, only you're such a smart cookie that by the time you reach the preplanned "test," it's like something a toddler could do. It's already pointless because your life experience has surpassed the planned assignment. In other words, you'd have a tough time matching your level of awareness to the lesson, unless you somehow knew every circumstance leading up to the lesson in your life. If you knew that before birth, then your life would be preplanned down to the exact detail and living would be merely "going thorough the motions" of predestination.

So, instead you might think, *Okay, so life is more flexible. Birth and death are irrelevant in the deeper levels where time isn't relevant. Maybe I can insert lessons on the fly, all through-out my physical life, in order to match my experience of now.*

If this is the case, then why would you plan lessons for yourself—what are you expected to learn, and who's grading the test? The word *lesson* implies that someone or something is going to evaluate and assess your performance. Who can do this, really, except yourself? The only consciousness who really knows you *is you.* Remember, of course, that you're as much a piece of Source as anything . . . and you're in a place of constant discovery and expression of who you are. So is it the you of yesterday, today, or tomorrow that's evaluating you? And if you suggest that it's the Greater You, then to what end?

Now, you may say, "Perhaps Source is critiquing my performance and has an ideal that I need to reach—maybe some combination of absolute peace, love, or charity that I'm supposed to someday embody."

Again, you then must ask, "To what end?" You're a fila-ment of Source energy. For Source to critique you, Source would be critiquing Itself—punishing or rewarding Itself—and seeking to make Itself into something else by molding Itself through suffering. So, does Source have an end goal for Itself? This is an intriguing question, but one that sug-gests that Source isn't already everything. It proposes that Source, too, is trying to grow into something else, and that there's a "something else" *outside Source* for it to grow into being—it's a circular argument.

The only way this idea of lessons can be true is if you feel that there's an external entity that grades all of life against some invisible code, and then creates elaborate systems for pushing people through this classroom to cre-ate more desirable contents in your soul. This suggests separation from Source and means that It had to create an inferior product which it then tries to perfect.

I think that we, as humans, have adopted this idea of lessons because we're applying our own human-scale game to the cosmic order. We go to school and we're graded, at work our bosses assess our performance, and even at home our parents and spouses expect us to follow their rules. We're always in situations of having to learn and be successful according to other people's rules, and so we want to apply the rules of our physical framework to the nonphysical.

So always be conscious of the fact that as you create experiences for yourself, you're already adding great value by seeing, expressing, and creating for Source. There's never a need to grade or compare these experiences with anything.

Perhaps you're thinking that coming to know the profundity of who you are is the point of this life, perhaps by attaining a deeper connection with Source. That may be true for you. In fact, I suspect that this may be one of my goals, as well as the aim of many humans. But consider that we all have different goals and motivations because of the unlimited creativity of Source. Might there be other goals we're completely unaware of? Further, is coming to be one with Source a goal, or more of an inevitability? Goals imply work and struggle. Inevitability implies release and enjoyment of the now, since this inevitability awaits.

Mastery Over Experiences

Of course, letting go of the idea of the need for harsh lessons doesn't mean you can't enjoy mastery over an experience. If you desire mastery over some part of your life, such as developing high self-esteem, then in order to create the curriculum for this, you might pre-act feelings around that goal: *I feel free of fear. I am worthy and powerful. I have so much value to add to the world. I am deserving.*

You'd then organize your life energies to bring you circumstances to explore these conditions. You might choose some difficult situations to encounter as part of learning to master self-worthiness, or you might choose to Flow in only positive experiences instead. It's of your *own choosing*. Nothing is forcing you through the same harsh mill as anyone else in the picture. Attaining personal mastery over an experience or quality is different from an externally graded lesson. Mastery implies a depth of understanding knowable only to the person experiencing it.

And, have you ever considered that you can learn just as much from happy, positive experiences as you can from miserable ones? A peaceful life can offer up subtleties not found in one with more turbulence. But, we seem to get caught up in this idea that we only really learn through tragedy and struggle, or that to become great at something, we need to pack in as many harsh situations as we can. But what of learning to love? What of admiring the beauty of a mountain range glowing in a sunset, or the iridescent blue of a desert sky? What of the delight of exploration and discovery of new things? What of learning to cultivate the values of honesty, love, and empathy in your children? This is a delight! There are so many other ways to gather experiences for us—for Source. Why should we elevate the troublesome and unhappy encounters as the most worthy?

All I ask is that *you ask yourself* why you rationalize the continual creation of unhappiness in your life by dressing it up as a noble life lesson to get through. Most likely, you're simply creating disharmony in your life because you've never learned how not to. The idea that life can be easy, that you can choose not to struggle, may seem foreign. And to be sure, you'll still encounter plenty of situations brought in by the people around you that will cause you grief—but let them be the ones creating trouble, while you take the smooth, easy path.

"Still," you might protest, "even if I accept this view, didn't I still choose all these hardships for myself? Didn't I preplan this? Isn't it in my 'chart' or something? Because I wouldn't have chosen all the crap in my life if there wasn't a good reason to go through it. It's got to make me a better person!"

These questions are just another variation of the "aren't I here to learn lessons?" theme. Here's the crux of the situation: to become a manifesting practitioner—and practice Flowdreaming—means you accept that life is fluid, changeable, and always full of possibility. Manifesting acknowledges that every second of every day you're putting out energetic desires of what you both hope *and* expect. You're laying down the road ahead of you a few feet a time, and the road can go anywhere. If you decide that you're not going to be poor anymore or that you're going to attract love in your life, you can't also say to yourself, "Yes, but it was in my chart that I'd suffer and have all this tragedy," or "I knew so-and-so and I would meet and have that relationship because of a past life." If that were true, then you might as well forget manifesting.

Manifesting Will Change Your Path

Let's look at one final example, and logically work it backward to see why this idea of having preplanned your life experiences dissolves once and for all after you enter the world of manifesting. Once you grasp this, you have the true power of creating in the now.

Say that before birth you planned a life where certain large events will appear—some positive (meeting your soul mate, having a great career) and some negative (having three really abusive marriages, then getting cancer).

When you're born, it turns out that you're a really smart gal. You had some good genes (preplanned, too, of course). You go to college, where you change and grow, and that's when the first "preplanned" guy (let's call him Man #1) enters your life. Oddly, you're too busy to really get into it with him, so that marriage disappears—oops, that wasn't according to plan.

Next, you graduate, and because you avoided that first ugly relationship, when Man #2 comes along, you don't have the same triggers that you would have had if you'd already trained yourself toward abuse through Man #1. Consequently, the relationship with Man #2 never gets off the ground and that marriage never happens either. So, hey, pass go—you're really cruising now! At this point, you're due for abusive Man #3. But wait, you've already effectively skipped ahead, like getting bumped up a grade. Would these preplanned experiences you already avoided really force you into circumstances with Man #3? Since they never occurred, you don't need that lesson anymore. Manifesting means that you're free at any point to change. So in this situation, a manifester would say, "Man #3 is going to be a terrific person!" and he would be. Similarly, she'd address cancer by continually pre-acting in her Flow: "I feel gloriously healthy. I treat my body well."

What happens to most of us is simply this: we enter so-called horrible experiences because we don't know any better. They aren't arranged at some specified time before birth, we aren't repaying mistakes from past lives, we aren't being punished for sinning, and we aren't actively creating horrible experiences through our focused intention.

Most of us are moving through life without any awareness of the energetic blueprints we're continually creating. We've never been told before that we can actively alter our futures, change our lives, and create things for ourselves using flowing templates of energy that underlie all life. We *could be* steering our lives within the graceful river of our internal Flow, moving with its current in a direction of ease and pleasure. But instead, most of us stumble through life oblivious to this idea and run into everything that comes our way—simply because we're not looking at what we're doing from an energetic, or manifesting, standpoint.

In reality, we repeat our mistakes over and over only because we become conditioned to their energy. For example, if you were raised around an alcoholic, you'll probably seek out a partner with the same or a similar affliction because that's what you've known—you're continually creating more of that energy state. You're not engaged in some deep karmic rebalancing with this person, and God isn't testing you. You're simply creating more of what you're used to. Like begets like.

If this example just rattled you, what it shows is that you'll need to examine the depth of your desire to learn to manifest, because you probably carry all sorts of dogma that will act as reins pulling you back from your true power. The more beliefs you have that lock you into preordained circumstances, the less power you give to the idea that you can remake your world at will.

I RAN UP AGAINST THIS WALL early on myself, and it hurt. I used to believe that much in my life was there through karma, or because I'd set up certain horrible experiences for myself so that I'd "purify" my soul to achieve higher levels of awareness as a result. I had many tidy explanations for why bad things happened, along with many rationales for why I had to go through certain traumas as a child. I also felt that I had the metaphorical "whip at my back" constantly forcing me through emotionally torturous experiences because I chose a particularly hard life in this "Earth school." Since I was an *A* student, I told myself that I'd selected the harder courses.

I was forced to throw away all these ideas, and the associated pride, one by one. It wasn't easy, and I tried to find ways to hang on to them whenever I could. What happened, though, is that every time I stubbornly held on to one, I found that my power to design my life diminished. I gave away my power to the beliefs that held me where I was, or supposedly "explained" my situation. Usually, my justification centered around my having to prove something, earn something, or be judged in a way that would allow the situation to finally pass. In other words, it was as if some other force would have to finally evaluate me and say, "Okay, good enough. Let her move on."

It was shocking when I finally saw through this explanation. Not only did I realize that my understanding of Source would never judge me in such a way, but I saw that this notion also carried through to the way we organize our whole society. Like I said already, if you please your boss or get an *A* on the test, you get a reward. If not, you'll be punished and have to do your work over. I had so many people or beings to please—no wonder I couldn't please *myself.*

This common way of looking at life is no accident; it's a result of biological conditioning in which human life evolved based on accomplishment. The first organisms that could breathe air and survive on land had an advantage because they escaped certain predators and were able to breed more easily. Apes that used tools to perform a task had a better chance of being healthy and producing more offspring like themselves. Accomplishment created a reward: *living one more day.*

In this day and age, we continue this by creating social and religious structures that also propagate this idea. But *must* this pattern of punishment and reward apply to our consciousness and spiritual life? I strongly doubt it; and if it does, it's a pattern that can be discarded as part of our next evolutionary step.

If you believe that every layer of yourself is enmeshed in even deeper layers of information (quantum data) and that manifesting merely means you access these deeper layers and rewrite them, then the whole question of "life lessons" becomes irrelevant. Why? Because you're writing your life on the fly—you're creating purely in the now, directing your life from this moment forward, based on the "you" that exists in this moment. Each second is already a pinnacle for you because you're more than you were a moment before.

Chapter 11

Life Shouldn't Be Fair

Right now you might be thinking, "It sounds like Flow-thinking justifies *everything*. If we're all just God having experiences, and we're gaining self-awareness from these experiences, then where does right or wrong fit in? Can it all just be *experience* without being called 'good' or 'evil'? Are you saying that God doesn't care *what* It experiences?"

The answer to these questions is both yes and no. Truly, when we look at this planet, we see a lot of misery: there's hunger, deprivation, illness, and mental anguish of untold measure. I know that whenever I hear of children living in squalor or in an abusive home, I feel a horrible, visceral reaction as I want to reach out and abolish every slum or unfit parent in the world. Just because God may not favor one particular experience over another doesn't mean that

I can't work to uphold what *I* feel is right and wrong. Still, I wonder, *Why would God allow this?*

Keep in mind that for God, all of life is in constant motion. The feelings of pain and despair are just some of the many millions of experiences we encounter. That some of us choose, or are born into circumstances that encourage, negative emotions is part of the landscape of God's experience. Humans are not the only active consciousness of God. We only *know* of ourselves, although many of us do understand that there are legions of other intelligences—besides plants, animals, and ecologies—all acting as expressions of God's eyes. (You may believe in angels, spirit guides, alien life, nonphysical entities, or "more aware" intelligences of all varieties that decorate our universe and the universes beyond.)

Our human condition has its particular flavor—one that tends toward misery and ignorance. It offers an unusual experience that's checkered with harsh, strong emotional encounters. Imagine a universe without that offering—much like not having Tabasco, chilies, hot sauce, or horseradish at a buffet. Some people wouldn't care, but some would.

Consider, too, that because you're part of this Earth experience now doesn't mean you're not somewhere, somehow simultaneously experiencing some very opposite way of living or being. In other words, perhaps a part of you is already existing in heaven where there's only love, and horrible emotions never reach you. As the age-old argument goes, would you even understand the beauty of that condition—perfect, constant, unremitting love—if you had no feeling of its opposite?

What I offer are ideas to consider as you call into question what you believe in, from the most fundamental point onward. I ask you to do this because I've found that to move away from unconscious creation, you must first become aware of the ties that bind you.

To return to the original question, "Where does right and wrong fit in the realm of Source's experiences?" it is truly up to you to decide what kind of experiences you want to have, and how many of those will create suffering for yourself or others. For God, everything you do is just more exploration of Its—your—Source self.

You May Be a Timeless Being, but Don't Expect Equality

You now recognize that as an eye of God, you're a timeless being, existing in a state of infinity. As a pinprick of consciousness housed in a human shell, you're part of a much larger system—both physically and nonphysically. Only part of your much broader awareness is focused inside your physical body.

You feel and look solid, because here and now matter has condensed in such a way that you have this "tool" of a body to move around and perform in within a three-dimensional world. It's like inhabiting a toy car so that you can play on a racetrack for a while. When you're done, you withdraw yourself from the car, but you haven't fundamentally changed.

So why does one person drive a new Porsche and the next drive a used Camry? You know the answer: life isn't fair. But *why* would it be designed like this? Why would the Flow allow so much inequality?

When you occupy this car—this body—you find yourself constrained by certain limitations, which helps create inequality. You come into a body with a certain fundamental set of rules in play—the common rules that ground us all into the same shared reality—as well as your particular rules that set up the basic playing field: your race, your socioeconomic class, the country and city you live in, and your body's physical and mental attributes to name a few. The rules make the game more difficult . . . and more interesting. If you choose easy ones—being born to a rich, white-collar family in a wealthy nation—then it might be like playing go fish, and your game may be easier in many respects. If you opt for harder, more complicated rules, such as coming into a body with a disability or an abusive family, then it's more like playing bridge or poker. You've raised the level of difficulty for yourself and may encounter many challenging situations.

The body, family, economic circumstance, and all other conditions surrounding our birth—even the country we're born in or the genes in our bodies that lay dormant—help set up the playing field of our particular experiences. We each arrive with a particular series of limitations, or "rules," for our game. While we might be timeless beings, we shouldn't expect equality. It won't be a fair game—and it shouldn't be—because we all want different experiences, and we're each playing this game with a different set of rules.

Some rules and limitations are coded in right from the start, such as what you arrive with: your genes, race, social class, and so on. But most of what you run into in life are just greater and lesser *possibilities*. For example, say that you choose to live in an area where there are floods. You accept that having a massive flood enter your experience is something that has a greater chance of coming to you. You aren't "manifesting" a flood and it wasn't preplanned, but you've created the *greater probability* for one by choosing to live where you do. Your playing field contains the possibility for floods where another person's doesn't. Clearly it's not fair, but it *is interesting.*

Or, let's say that your body predisposes you to a certain disease. The genes were there as part of your initial manifestation, and as you go through life, you unknowingly trigger them, causing the illness to develop. Why did you unknowingly do this? Well, perhaps you've been living unaware that you even had the gene. Maybe you felt great stress, and coupled with an environmental contaminate, this was just what that gene needed in order to kick on. You didn't intend any of this and weren't even aware of the possibility; however, like most people, you believe that your body does its own thing and you can't control it, so you manifest or accept whatever comes along. So the first domino has been tipped over, and a series of events were put in motion bringing on the illness.

We all have many things occurring for us every day that run along such invisible paths of creation, like the above example of illness. None of us can "see" ahead to know what's going to happen in the next moment. The next moment is constantly in play, as many trillions of possibilities interact to produce results in our lives. The key is to think about whether or not you've offered these possibilities any direction or guidance. Have you set ground rules? How are you thinking and living to guide the results? What's your default mode set at?

Let's inject some awareness into this process. First, state a ground rule that's meant to alter your default mode: "I don't know if I have a tendency toward this illness or not. It doesn't matter, because I'm continually healthy and vibrant. That illness is not part of my state of being." Now, because we know it's best when we marry the invisible to the visible—pairing your energy template with physical action—we support this assertion by exercising, eating well, and refraining from doing things that cause the illness, such as not smoking if our concern is cancer.

Here we've executed a script of sorts, like a computer programmer writing code. This programmer has said, "Here's what I want to happen [being healthy]. I'm going to nudge things in that direction by writing some code into the energy language of Flow that will continually create health."

So you input this script. You, as a piece of consciousness, an eye of God experiencing life, have said, "I choose this experience." This is your intention, or manifesting desire, for today.

However, the days go by and you forget. You begin worrying about the illness again. In fact, someone you know has it, so it's now heavy on your mind. Every time you think about it, you're filled with dread, and as a result, you're filling the Flow—life energy around you—with this very potent emotional connection to the sickness. This thinking is, in effect, unraveling and writing over the code you previously wrote. And, of course, you're completely unaware that this is happening, since you're so involved in your worry that you don't even realize what your thinking is doing to you. You're exuding two conflicting energy desires for health and sickness—alternately pushing cancer away and then pulling it to you. The tipping point comes when you allow your body to become stressed and ill—because you've forgotten all about the potent, counterbalancing Flowdreaming work—and the energy moves toward the illness.

This is not an optimistic scenario. Yet it's what you do, in a million ways, with all kinds of situations in your life that you feel you both don't want and didn't choose. Even so, as you embark on this new experience (that of learning to be a manifesting practitioner), you'll begin a lifelong shift that will allow you, more and more as each day and year passes, to more effectively create within your life. Life may not be fair, but you *can* even things out a bit.

Manifesting is not an overnight skill, any more than becoming an athlete is. You must practice, be enthused, and remain positive and confident about your potential. Examine all your beliefs and toss out the ones that no longer serve you, and then face the scary notion that with such skill comes great power. You won't be able to blame others any longer or say "That's life" or "Shit happens."

The goal is to develop guidelines that harness the energies of your life into pathways that allow for more and more enjoyable experiences. You'll create a template that defines what you hope, expect, and experience. Your default mode will remain charged up and defined, automatically allowing in experiences you want while closing the door to the ones you don't. You'll be better able to handle those limitations you chose to play with in this game, whether these are physical handicaps, difficult family members, or even your own character flaws. Once you do this, life will no longer seem *frustratingly* unfair; it will be *splendidly* and *perfectly* unfair.

If There's No Life Purpose, Then What Are We Here For?

At some point, as the world of physical entertainment wears thin, we start to look around and question, "Is this all there is?" The game can become both beautiful and awe inspiring—a thing of marvelous complexity—yet we're tired of working within the same old rules, within the same confines, doing the same things over and over. We begin to say, "There must be something more." Sometimes this comes to us like a slap in the face, as we wake up one morning and groan, "Every day is the same. Surely I don't have to do all this over again. It never ends."

This is the point when many people turn to religious or spiritual practice. Or when they begin to look at all the tools they heretofore had for shaping their life, and say, "I've been using my shovel and pail to build my sand castle and all the things in my world, but I know I'm missing a tool. There must be something else!"

Many of us mistake this for the feeling of needing a life purpose or finding the "one true path" to God. We feel the shifting and churning, and we run around seeking someone to put us in the right direction again. We hate this feeling of unease, especially when it makes us question so much of what we've been happily believing until now.

And yet our life purpose and spirituality is in the making, moment by moment. Your life purpose is the same as everyone else's: to explore, taste, and enrich your consciousness with whatever delights you can discover here on Earth. And "delights" doesn't imply a hedonistic, selfish rampage.

If developing your psychic skills turns you on, then do so. If building a thriving, successful company makes you feel good, then go for it; and if having children and watching them grow into their own repositories of experience feeds your soul, then have them. All the while continually look around and decide what other interests you're here to explore. What feels good? Usually, what feels good also benefits others in some way as well—for instance, you might do good work, raise fine kids, and take care of your elderly parents. You aren't trying to be a do-gooder, but you find that the best emotion comes to you from the happiness of others.

YOU BRING TO EVERY SITUATION your unique, individual perspective. Call this your "essence," your "Flow," or your "perception"—it's the sliver of Source looking out and encountering life through the lens of your particular human experience. This lens colors everything your own shade, like rose-colored glasses; or maybe it's purple and green with spots, or golden with streaks of bronze. After all, each of us is purposefully unique. Not one other person thinks like you, feels like you, or is you in any way. Isn't that amazing?

What's more, we all go through the same repetitive experiences (wake, eat, work, play, interact with others), yet we each turn out so differently. We move in waves of similarity with others (we join political parties with like-minded people and form religions and whole cultures with others of similar attitudes and beliefs!), but as with snowflakes or daisies, none of us are a carbon copy of another.

And why would God do this?

God is an artist and a scientist. God is a building with a thousand doors into it, and It is eager for us to create new doors every day to show Itself more of what It is. Think about this: if Source energy weren't completely enamored with creativity, artistry, and exploration, then our world would surely be radically different. Perhaps we'd only have one sex, or the colors of our world might only be blues and browns. Such a variety of species wouldn't be necessary, either. A few would do, preferably all very similar. And why three dimensions? How about only two? For that matter, let's get rid of this marvelous universe and all the stars and black holes within it.

If we're here to strictly serve a moral code that ultimately judges our worthiness for an afterlife, then that could easily be done under a much narrower set of circumstances. I mean, come on, the playing field keeps changing! A man in A.D. 1200 had to wrestle with whether or not to steal vegetables from his neighbor's garden, but a man today must decide if stem-cell research is morally tenable. Why give us such ambiguous options for mistake or development? Why not keep the playing field even and judge apples to apples for all eternity? Why let us grow at all?

If God weren't a master artist, enamored with creation, then our palette would be greatly limited. We wouldn't grow or be on an arc of continual expansion and evolution.

For Source, the more differences there are among us, the better. The greater the variety, the more opportunity there is to see and experience more, see Itself through additional lenses of perception, and to know Itself through expanded means. God is the ultimate creator, and Source's achievement is all that we are . . . and even more that we don't see.

A fundamentalist of *any* religion will read this and feel shock and revulsion. To this person, or anyone with a hardened belief system, God had to choose the "right" way to see Itself and condemn the rest. God is only one way, and not another.

What a limited God! That's a God with no imagination, no creative energy, and no appetite to see Itself in all Its wonder. God didn't forge a tightly controlled game with no variation. Stagnant systems don't survive. Our universe, on the other hand, thrives with variety.

Growth Through Perception

As an aspect of Source, you're here to explore creation and find yourself through all the physical and non-physical means at your disposal. And by "find yourself," I don't mean that you're lost or disconnected. Rather, you find yourself through your moment-by-moment encounter with yourself and others. You *discover* yourself. And there's always more to find and learn about, since you're continually adding to yourself each second like a blanket being knitted—the stitches of your existence flying into place as you accumulate experience and develop into more. *With every encounter, you are adding to the sum of selfhood.* Consider that with every moment ticking by, you're acquiring something you didn't have a moment ago: a bit of time in which something happened. This "something that happened"—whether it's a thought that flew through your head, a phone call, an absorption of something on TV, or even a profound realization about yourself—is added to the collection of experiences that is you. You've grown—you've expanded.

So why, then, do we have such *repetition* in our existence? When this Flowthinking understanding of life first came to me, the question of repetition was one of the first things that popped up to resist the idea. If we're involved in continual exploration and creation, why do we as a species all experience the same emotions—such as love, hate, jealousy, joy—over and over again? Why do the vast majority wake in the morning, sleep at night, eat, and eliminate in an utterly mundane cycle? And why do millions of us suffer and die in infancy, before our lives even begin? Why do millions of others of us live long past that point when life is meaningful to us? Why do millions have to suffer like that? Wouldn't one or a few such experiences be enough? *Why is humanity so gosh darn repetitive?*

Consider the ocean waves again. Every moment, day and night, the waves crash onto ocean shores around the world, without end. From a larger perspective, the action is repetitious; however, from within each wave, the view changes dramatically. Each wave is made from different molecules of water, so the volume and flow of water within it is unique. Every wave scoops different particles of sand from the ocean floor as it rolls in and displaces different shells and bits of seaweed and fish. Once the perspective changes, so does the viewpoint, and each "repetitious" wave instead becomes a cosmos of individuality.

So it is for us. We all appear as identical as raindrops, repetitive in our common emotions and the shared experiences we build into our lives—but within each of these experiences is a universe of differences.

Sure, our common biology gives us templates or parameters for this life: we're driven toward pleasure and away from pain. It's as if Source set up ground rules to keep us all within the same general reality so that relationships could in fact occur. But within these rules that our physical world and biology dictate, we're given free reign. Our choices are without end.

Part III

Musings

*"For an artist, white space represents
the unmanifested."*

In Part III, we'll explore various aspects of Flow energy in our lives. I give you each of these chapters as a small essay around a particular subject. Each subject has been important to me at one point or another in my journey, whether I'm discussing the influence of fear in our lives or how our environment impacts us. These essays aren't especially well organized, and they may seem to jump around; it's just that each one excited my interest at one time or another, and I believe some may strike chords with you, too. Enjoy.

Chapter 12

Energy—What Is It?

The winds outside my home carry what feels like an electrical current. In Southern California, we call these hot, dry winds "Santa Anas," and every year they appear without fail, curling in from the desert in the east.

When they're blowing, people around here are more edgy than normal. There's an excitement in the air—a need to move, a restlessness. If we accidentally rub our feet along the carpet, we'll send a current of static electricity into the next conductive object we encounter. So we keep our space from each other—knowing that we're wonderful conductors of electricity—since a shock comes with almost every brief contact as we casually grasp a friend's arm or kiss a child's head.

All human beings everywhere *are* wonderful conductors—not just of static electricity, but for all kinds of transmitted currents. When we grasp a radio antenna, the reception improves; so, too, for TV antennae. Our bodies have the ability to act as receivers for many kinds of natural waves, whether radio, electrical, or other as-yet-unnamed forms of energetic communication.

As I think about what good antennae and conductors we are, I watch the palm tree outside my home bend, its fronds blowing in the charged wind. I know that science has clearly identified many forms of waves and energy—it's discovered cosmic waves, sound waves, light waves, and more. Biologists have explained how the palm tree is right now converting sunlight (waves of heat and color) into food, thus making energy to grow with. Physicists have identified many means of making electrical current, and they've developed numerous ways of extracting electricity from sources unimaginable—nuclear, oil, biomass, wave action, geothermal, and more. When we talk about *energy* in science, we usually mean specifically some kind of power source. When we talk about *vibration* or *waves* in science, we refer to those that communicate data or charge.

But in metaphysical circles, we use these terms *energy, waves,* and *vibration* pretty loosely. We speak of vibration and energy, knowing that we're referring to something utterly intangible. It's as if we, the terrific conductors that we are, somehow know that there are more than just the known currents of energy coursing through us. There are other energies—still unidentified by mainstream science—that we can feel in our veins.

Talk to an acupuncturist, and they might call these "meridians." Ask any energy healer, and you'll discover even more names for the ribbons of body energy that flow through us and make up our energetic field.

A master of the internal martial arts, such as tai chi, qigong, Xiang Yi, or bagua might discuss "chi"; a spiritual practitioner or psychic might talk about an "aura" or "bodily energy field"; and a Yogi will tell you about "prana" or perhaps "kundalini."

A scientist will remind us that we're made from spinning atoms, or quantum data, which are appearing and disappearing in fragments of time and space so small as to be unimaginable, but which collectively creates the cohesive illusion of physical solidity, making us much like an image on an old flickering filmstrip that's jerkily flashing in and out of existence as this data spins and flows through us in predictable patterns.

My point is that we seem to know that we're not just composed of a fundamental energy, but that this force makes up an interior map of ourselves, much like the blueprint for a house. Within this map inside each of us there are tides, pathways, or flowing roadways of data, and there are many points where information is received and processed or expelled and communicated. When one of us encounters another, then like that spark of static electricity that jumps between us, our energy fields likewise communicate an instant read of each other.

In the soup of energy at our basis, defined edges become blurred and potentially nonexistent. We maintain our distinction much as a person in a room remains both distinct from the room yet still part of it. This room is part of the house, so the person is—temporarily, at least—also part of the house. The house is a unit in the neighborhood, so the person, room, and house are as well. The neighborhood is part of the earth, so you are as well.

Aliens looking down on us from space might not see us as individuals, but instead think, *Oh, what an interesting thing, this neighborhood. Look at all the parts inside it. Each part does its own unique thing.* How long would it take them to distinguish the individual energy signature of us—the individuals—as important, or singularly independent? Or, it's just as likely that they'd perceive our spinning masses of atomic energy and fail to see beyond this to our larger, more cohesive bodies. These aliens may attempt to contact the individual atoms within us, unaware or unable to see the larger mass that is us.

Perspective is the only thing that allows us to distinguish our defined edges or boundaries, and it's what allows us to see individuals within larger systems. Our bodily point of view doesn't allow us to see the energy that flows through us at a deeper level (although some special individuals do seem to feel it, such as healers). This blindness causes us to assume that these deeper levels aren't there, or, even if they are, they're fundamentally unimportant. Moreover, we don't just ignore our *own* internal flow, we completely overlook the energy states of everything around us.

IT'S STRANGE HOW WE DO SO MUCH NAVEL-GAZING that we often forget that we aren't the only creatures with this internal energetic landscape. The animals and plants that live with us likewise share this internal link to these fundamental energies.

But what about rocks, mountains, and seas; and what of the earth itself? Wouldn't it make sense for all life, from the smallest scale to the largest ecosystems, to share in the same energetic blueprints?

We're conditioned to think in terms of finite, concrete objects. Except for a few scientists, we don't often think of systems, or combinations of objects, as having characteristics of cohesion or a raison d'être. But if you expand your thinking to include something as large as a river valley as having a kind of "body" with flows of energy coursing through it, you begin to look at everything differently. The river in the valley conducts not just water but delivers an energy of sustenance to the larger organism of the valley, much as our own circulatory systems deliver blood to our body, along with life and vitality.

Once you recognize this perspective, you're beginning to think in terms of *patterns* of energy. So the supposedly "dead" rock that sits on the bottom of the river in this valley is dead only in its ability to hold and express consciousness—but it's nonetheless tied in to the greater organism, just as your gallbladder is tied to you. This river valley is energetically connected to everything within it, as the energy components of everything in the valley are sloshed together in the deeper levels of being. They appear separate to your level of perspective—but shift your point of perception, and the landscape changes.

Carry this further, and you begin to widen your thinking from discrete objects to the systems of interaction they have. As people, we organize ourselves into cultures, and each culture carries very specific energy signatures. Some are violent and dominant, while others are peaceful and receptive. Imagine these collected expressions of every individual in these cultures forming a larger net of energy—an energy pattern of expression.

From here, you can start thinking about circulating systems as also having a pattern to them—such as the circulation of money. Imagine that money is both an object—you can hold currency in your hand—while it also has an abstract quality that we call "value." Value may be backed by money, but value itself is more like a flow of people's feelings. My home isn't valuable because it's made from dollar bills stacked together as bricks—its valued in context to the neighborhood its in, its age, its square footage, and so on. People's feelings about the desirability of all these things is what shapes the value. Because of these factors, the value is always changing—growing or decreasing. Viewing money or value as a concept or energy condition rather than an object lets you begin to sense its true vibration.*

Money then becomes a river of energy, colored and shaped by the billions of people who are constantly adding their feelings to its vibration. I often imagine it as a giant net over the world, connected to each individual, with some connections minutely small (such as the one to that person living on less than one dollar a day in the developing world) to huge rushing infalls (such as the waterfall of wealth connecting icons such as Microsoft's Bill Gates).

This net is a pipeline of constantly moving energy that's being distributed and redistributed, and originated, consumed, and reoriginated. So while I may not be able to physically go to the bank and withdraw a million actual dollars, in this deeper state where I'm connected to the river of money energy, I can allow my field to interact with this deep well of wealth. I can virtually swim in the million dollars, pull it to me, or put any kind of feeling or emotion onto it that I desire.

Looking at the opposite end of money, we find poverty, or the lack of value and abundance. (When I touch the feeling of poverty's energy with my mind, it feels dry and dusty, wizened and empty.) Lack occupies its own river of

---

*For a comprehensive look at the presence of wealth in our lives, look to my book-and-CD set *The Flowdreaming Prosperity Challenge* at **Flowdreaming.com**.

being that we each tap into. While we probably have more than a bowl of rice to eat today, we could still be tapping this energy of restraint and deficiency in another area of our lives.

You can extrapolate from here to other concepts, such as thoughts, situations, conditions, and feelings. You name it, and you can find an energy signature for it, whether it's physical or nonphysical. Think of anything in your life, and you'll immediately recognize the energy or vibration of it. Anger has a signature. My tennis shoes have a signature. The relationship I have with my boss is composed of a current of information or data, which contains all of our interactions and myriad potentialities. My thought about writing this sentence carries an energy fingerprint, which you're accessing as you take in the information I've just conveyed. You and I are engaged in an energy exchange— even though I wrote this long before now—while you read these words. It's a miracle of energy exchange that you're able to take the gist of my thinking from these written words, in a kind of "delayed impact" of exchange from me to you.

I realize, of course, that none of these assertions may ultimately be provable from our physical perspective. Like that fish trying to intuit what's outside of the water, forever unable to access the outside air, we're trapped within certain physical parameters that constrict our knowledge— for now.

This is why I'm more of a philosopher than a scientist. By choosing a philosophy that tells me that not just all of God's creatures, but all of *everything,* is based on a deeper fundamental energy structure, I can see life as a field of infinite potential. The trick is to stop perceiving a thought as merely a thought, and start viewing it as shooting arrow of energy. We must stop seeing an interaction between two people as merely a physical encounter, but instead see it as a Flow of energy between two organisms with much of the data transfer taking place at levels deeper than the physical.

As you begin to see the world in terms of these energy patterns, of Flows or signatures, your ability to manifest will increase. You'll go beyond just understanding the process intellectually as you begin to feel the patterns and Flows in place within all things.

Chapter 13

Learn to Feel the Energy

Recently, my family and I spent the day at SeaWorld. After hours of watching the killer whales, dolphins, and barracuda, the only animal that stayed in my mind was the quiet, gray octopus.

This octopus was kept alone in a small aquarium in a dark room. It kept unfurling its long tentacles against the glass and looking at me with one beady eye. Without realizing I'd done so, I found myself mentally inside this creature's energy field and could actually *feel* the octopus. It felt dulled and primitive, and pushed by urges it didn't have the self-awareness to name. Its sense of imprisonment was almost heartbreaking. It had no concept of *cage*, or *glass*, or *tank*, yet it contained a driving, fundamental need to *go*. It seemed unaware that it couldn't take off to explore, swim, and do whatever it is that octopuses do. But I could definitely tell that urge to *move* was strong, while the inability to do so was constant—together these created a dismal kind of madness, and it made me feel horrible.

You know by now that it's not so hard to enter another being's energy field. In fact, it's probably harder *not* to enter. A few feet of water and a piece of glass are no match for the energy state. We inadvertently enter others' fields all the time. Remember the last time you went to an enclosed mall, and soon after you arrived you felt tired, distracted, and unable to focus? You were very likely intercepting the random energies of all the other people there who were feeling confused, overwhelmed, or unsure of what to buy. Whenever I realize that I'm in this state, I immediately leave the environment I'm in and tell myself to try again another day—when I'm less susceptible to being zapped by the dull, lost fields of those around me.

When I go anywhere else that has crowds, such as a theme park or a fair, I often feel a variation on this: instead of feeling confused and foggy, I begin to feel irritable, draggy, and a little compulsive. I spend money on things that I wouldn't normally buy, and my patience wears thin as people bump into me or walk too close. The energies of all the different people at the park begin to absorb and mix into everyone else's, and a collective Flow is created that each individual becomes attuned to—whether they're aware of it or not.

Even as you spend time with your family in your own home, you'll find yourself reacting to their energy fields—or Flows—and assimilating them into your own. When you enter a house in which two people have been arguing, the Flow of that home has been impacted with that energy and you can feel the heavy, upset "vibe" surrounding you.

If you aren't aware that this is happening, you can easily take in this energy from others and begin to feel nervous and upset yourself. In homes with very dominant personalities, you can become completely submerged in those other personalities' energies and you may wonder, *What is wrong with me?* Really, it isn't even you—you've just taken on another person's Flow, much like putting on their coat. It is *not* you.

Luckily, you can learn to distinguish your own Flow from the energy of others. One way that I mastered this ability was to practice feeling exactly what other people's Flows felt like—and I don't mean feeling their aura. It's more like looking into their mind (but not trying to probe it as with telepathy) and feeling their personality and thoughts as a combined whole. (Sometimes, though, you *do* accidentally enter their thoughts.) As your skill grows, you'll begin to sense a person in *motion* in their lives, and sense all the energy conditions that surround them. You're probably able to tap in and see the unfolding of the energies in their life.

To practice, it's best to begin with nonhumans. Go to a zoo, beach, or forest; and find an animal to focus on. Stare at this creature (perhaps not in the eyes, since that is a signal of aggression for many animals) and allow your mind to flow into it. You can use the trick of displacing your vision so that you imaginatively "see" out this animal's eyes. Ask with your emotions, *How do you feel? Hungry? Bored? Alert?* Try to understand what it's feeling at this moment.

This experience has yielded the most alien feelings I've ever had in that I've received impressions and emotions that were so outside our human repertoire that I couldn't even name them; my thoughts have been almost unprocessable. When you try it, you might feel something that's primal in a way that your more-evolved brain will have a hard time decoding.

After you're successful with animals, start working with people. When you feel the Flow of human beings, you sense more than just their mental or emotional state, you sense the waves of Flow they're traveling forward on. You can, of course, just go in and feel their current energy state—such as what healers or telepaths might do—but to sense their Flows, extend your mind into them as moving beings traveling forward.

When I help individuals, I often recognize their Flows as moving washes of light that convey huge amounts of information—not just about their past and future, but about the "gear" they're in, so to speak. Some people are stuck in neutral or have braked, while others are going so fast and frenzied that there's chaos and confusion in their Flow and their lives. As I sense a person's Flow, I feel their personality, thoughts, and their life's collected "essence" as well as all the events and situations surrounding them.

You can take this further still by feeling the Flows of conditions or situations. Practice sensing the Flow of the following energy states, which are just a sampling. There are many to experience, but these offer insights that may feel unique:

agreement	connection
argument	courage
beauty	dirtiness
circulation	disconnection
cleanliness	disorder
confrontation	disturbance

fear	order
freedom	poverty
health	satisfaction
imprisonment	stagnation
management	stealth
notoriety	ugliness
obscurity	wealth

The Energy of Fear

As I write these words, my five-year-old daughter is resting in the living room with a 104.4-degree fever. As I'll find out later in the night, it will eventually inch up to over 105. I've been a wreck with worry, and I wonder—as I always do every time my children become ill—why she has to go through this. How come I have to worry? Why is it necessary for our wonderful bodies to get so sick? And I also question why she would have allowed this in; did my daughter manifest this illness?

It's funny how my mind can turn over this same question time after time, because I know the answer perfectly well. Of course my daughter didn't intentionally create this for herself; just like all of us, she lives in a world of creation in which the Flows of others are always merging and mingling with her own—and viruses, like some people, don't respect boundaries.

The body processes pathogens and creates antibodies to them with predictable regularity. It does this to keep its immune system attentive and responsive so that it has the defenses to fight whatever other scarier viruses may come its way. My daughter's body is already churning out antibodies and developing resistance to this current strain of flu.

We live in agreement with our physical world—in agreement with our bodies and the environment that surrounds us. In this agreement, we accept certain rules to participate in physical life. We accept that exercise makes us healthier, and diet soda does not. We accept that our bodies have a delicate balance with the outside world and that they do a daily dance with the many other variety of bacteria, viruses, and life of all kinds that they encounter. Sometimes, even plagues appear, like wildfires in a forest, as part of a natural rhythm. It does not make it any easier.

If my daughter or I were perhaps sufficiently advanced in manifesting, one of us might be able to do something as miraculous as stopping the illness with the power of a thought, much as people have caused cancers and other deadly illnesses to vanish. But neither of us can comprehend the power of what that would mean—to instantly cure oneself—since our disbelief helps keep it from ever happening. This is one of my glass ceilings: the limits of my belief include the idea that while I can influence the resistance of her body by working directly with her own energy system, it will ultimately take rest, love, and practical approaches involving lots of fluids and ibuprofen for her to hustle through this quickly. I believe she possesses a great inner strength that will get her through most things, and she believes this about herself, too. Still, I have been exuding fear and worry almost continually for hours . . . and this concerns me as much as her fever.

So as I spend the evening panicking over my daughter's fever, I realize that what I'm offering both of our Flows is fear. While my thoughts are rooted in fear, I'm not generating healthful, restorative thoughts. I remind myself of this, and then I decide that I have to wrestle myself into being more positive and subdue the fear with strong conscious effort. I *make* myself feel that she'll be fine. I'm alert and responsive, and I know what warning signs to look for. I'll also be up every three hours throughout the night with a thermometer, but I refuse to generate any more fear for her sake.

Fear is an invasive energy that robs you of power. But, in its earliest appearance, fear is your friend because it alerts you to a potentially dangerous situation: Alert! Look out for the hot stove! Watch out for that speeding car! Pay attention to this fever! But after the initial warning, it hangs around like an old boyfriend in your apartment. It steals your next potential move from you, which is to correct the situation through optimism and practical means.

Since I began writing this, my daughter's temperature has momentarily dipped; she's now demanding crackers and chocolate milk. I'm relieved, but more than this, I'm glad to have found something to hang my hope on tonight—that she was coherent even at 104.4 and that she was drinking water and eating Popsicles.

It's not much, but when you're gripped with fear, you have to find even the smallest thing to help you turn the corner. When I exude confidence that all will be well, I color the air around me with the belief that my thoughts are impacting the situation at hand.

Now that I've changed my thinking, I take confidence in knowing that I have a practical plan, and I feel relief that the ibuprofen has made a dent of few degrees—102.5 doesn't look so bad to me now. And when I see my daughter give me a handwritten note that says, "I louv Mome," my joy is overwhelming.

All this leads me to send more of the vibration I want to feel in our home tonight, and when I specifically

Flowdream that my little one is feeling vibrantly healthy, I send much more power into the energies. I feel health, I feel well. I feel Flow.

I'M REMINDED OF AN EVENT from years ago when I spent a day feeling sick and vomiting through the night until nothing was left in my stomach—and still I vomited until bright yellow bile came out. In the morning, I called my mom and told her that I thought something might be really wrong; luckily we reached the hospital just as I went unconscious.

Four days went by as the apparently grossly inexperienced doctor tried to figure out what was wrong. Never mind that my lower right side was hurting or that I was vomiting and fevered. He treated me for a kidney infection that wasn't there. Finally, another doctor stepped in and ordered an ultrasound. It was clear: a ruptured appendix. However, by then the illness had spread and my blood was teeming with E coli. The appendix had developed gangrene and my colon had peritonitis; in other words, I had a raging, life-threatening infection. The hard-core antibiotics that I was required to take made me foam at the mouth, and I even hallucinated that I was falling through the hospital walls.

However, at no point did I think that I was going to die from this—despite how critical the situation got. Death never entered my consciousness; I *knew* I was going to get better.

A week later, as a more experienced doctor was attending to my still-open and draining surgical wound, we had a talk about what had happened. "You know," he told me, "I'm not worried about you. You're going to be okay. But I have another patient who's younger than you. Her appendix didn't even rupture, but she isn't doing well. She's so worried . . . it's not good."

I thought it was really strange that this man had so little concern for me and so much for this girl with a much lesser sickness. Only years later did I make the connection: as with many healers, whether alternative or traditional, he "sensed" the gravity of this girl's physical and mental states as well as my own. He knew that my attitude, along the Flow of healing that I was exuding, was going to carry me to safety, whereas her fear was endangering her life. The doctor was feeling the Flow of life that we were each perched on, like a sailor with his finger to the wind.

THE MESSAGE TO TAKE FROM THESE TWO EXAMPLES is that fear is one of the most powerful emotions of all. In your toolbox that you use to shape the Flow energies with, it's the giant hacksaw—and while it can do a lot of damage, some people can carve ice sculptures from hacksaws. Fear can be handled with power and precision, and "controlled" by converting its raw power into any other emotion you wish to pre-act into your Flow. To do this, you must simply find the raw Flow, or energy, that fear is made from. Pretend that fear is white paint to which black dye is being added. Grasp the white paint before the particular energy "color"—the fear color—is laid in. Also, search around for the strong, overwhelming "push" that tipped you deep into that fear. This "push" is the drive of the energy.

As you become a more experienced manifesting practitioner, you'll find this "core stuff" that fear is made from with greater ease. You can then transfigure this energy into any other feeling you desire—such as powerful healing, confidence, or gratitude that the fear-inducing situation has passed. For many, just knowing that you can alter the substance of fear into a new emotion is a revelation.

The Energy of Place

I live about 20 miles from a nuclear reactor that provides power for our region. In their great wisdom, the planners for this facility decided that positioning it almost directly on top of a major earthquake fault line was a good strategy.

Living so near to this time bomb has always made me uneasy. Now, I didn't have any part in creating this situation, and I won't have any part in creating the next major earthquake, either. So if some terrible tragedy were to happen, to what extent will I have manifested this into my reality?

We may ask ourselves this type of question all the time, especially regarding mass tragedies such as floods, firestorms, airplane crashes, wars, or bombings. Did the people who died, we wonder, collectively "choose" this? Why would they do that? This is a valid argument against the practice of manifesting and creating our reality.

What I've learned through the years is that wherever we are, there's a set of potentials in play. Some are wonderful, and some are distrastous. In my case, the disastrous ones include earthquakes, fires, nuclear meltdown, avian-flu pandemic, hantavirus, terrorist bombings, tidal waves, and a host of lesser and more common threats such as car wrecks and pneumonia. Each of these exists as a potential—like an underground stream of energy that could erupt into the physical if given the right circumstances.

By deciding to live here, I've "consented" to these possibilities by placing myself in proximity to them.

All places contain dangerous possibilities. And to purposely avoid them, I suspect that I'd need to keep myself in a state of utmost attunement, always holding my most perfect health and happiness in mind. Bringing back the coin analogy, I'd have to couple that with action and seek to remove all those troubling parts of my location as well. What a task! So, like everyone else, I accept the energetic possibilities inherent to where I live.

When you select an environment, always remember that it's just like selecting a mate: your city or town or country offers you certain freedoms and limitations, and it comes with its own potential for disaster. Sometimes we forget that we're not living on a island of our own making. Every encounter you have is an exchange with the energies around you. You make agreements every moment with your environment, too, accepting in the sunlight, the traffic, the density of people in the streets, the potential to be snowed in one day or caught in a blizzard without electricity the next. You may not have *chosen,* per se, to be trapped in your home during a wildfire, but you chose to live where this potential was part of your environment, and by extension a part of you. You chose to live with the potential that this would become a reality in your life, so you could have that encounter to add to your collection of experiences, and by so doing, understand how you, as God, would behave in that interesting set of circumstances.

SPEAKING OF YOUR ENVIRONMENT, your immediate surroundings, whether home or work, also heavily influence your Flow. As an example, a man recently called in to my radio show who was hoping to create some romance in his life. I didn't bother to ask him how long he'd been without a partner, or even what had happened in his past to create such a lack. Instead, as we spoke I immediately had a sense that this guy was somehow bland and flat—as if the "color" of his Flow had somehow been washed away.

I told him, "You know what? You feel so beige to me, Michael. It's like this feeling of 'boringness' has so surrounded you so that you're almost not there. How could a woman find you? You don't stand out. It's like all I see around you is tan, tan, tan. Do you drive a tan car?" I asked.

Michael laughed nervously and admitted, "Yes." He was driving it as he called me.

Michael's environment was as dry as a sandy creek bed; it lacked life. So how do you put *life* back in? I was struck by how his Flow showed its state of being as a color . . . one that evoked a feeling of humdrum boredom. So I told Michael to get some artwork that featured bright and swirling colors with bold strokes, such as paintings of the sidewalk cafés of Paris. I told him that if he didn't like that kind of art, he should get something he *did* like that was brilliant and full of vibrancy—its energy needed to be bound in the intensity of the colors, brushstrokes, and textures.

"Energy attracts like energy," I explained to Michael, "and utter desolation is showing itself all around you in your undecorated home; boring, tan car; and lack of a zesty, spicy love life."

Talking to him made me think about how our immediate surroundings profoundly affect us, and vice versa. It's no secret that artists always seem to congregate in the most interesting downtown neighborhoods or exotic islands, taking inspiration for their work from everything in their surroundings. As creatures of energy, we're compelled to seek environments that complement our natures.

I'm sure you've walked into businesses before and seen the rows and rows of drab cubicles. When energy is contained, boxed, and constricted in a kind of base functionality (as in so many mundane office settings), it's no wonder that the employees reflect this atmosphere in their own repetitive, mind-numbing work.

Years ago when I was the publisher of a magazine, I was able to spend time at our local newspaper—one of the larger ones in the U.S.—and being inside their building was incredibly stimulating. While cubicles ruled the interior layout, each employee had decorated his or hers so that almost all of the cubicle walls were covered with personal effects that blended into a sea of objects and colors. The work spaces of these layout artists, writers, and editors were stacked with clippings, stories, books, memorabilia, trinkets, photos, and anything else they'd collected in pursuit of a story or through their years at the paper. People's desks were overflowing with snippets of information or objects, and on the news floor, the energy was likewise abuzz with threads of potential. Their interior space perfectly reflected the nature of their work, which I'm sure also suited the energy signature of their personalities.

The point of my telling you this is to get you to think about your surroundings. Are they purely functional, or only half attended to? Are they cramped and crowded with so many things from your past, that you can hardly move into your future? Or are they stimulating and complementary to your nature?

When you're living within your Flow, you can use your surroundings as yet another medium of energy to program. When Michael adds color to his environment, for example—whether by tacking up some interesting prints to his walls, changing his screen saver, or buying a flashy red car—he's creating energy patterns around him that will begin to reflect his desires.

Practitioners of feng shui and other philosophies that describe the energetic space around us will recognize this approach. But for most of you, the idea of working from the outside (physical) in to reshape an aspect of your inner life is an unusual idea.

When I look around my house, I see a comfortable home with many bright colors and interesting objects. I've tried to create feelings of comfort, creativity, and beauty because I want these energies active in my Flow; so as life moves me forward, I can experience these conditions everywhere in my life.

Your particular desires may be different from my own, but the point is for you to see that having continuity in all your energy spaces is critical. Your home, work space, and self will all move in tandem with the same energies that will help cultivate the emotions you want in your whole life.

Think about your own surroundings again right now. Is there a disconnect? Is your home half furnished? Now think about your life: Do you lack a partner or a satisfying career? Is your work space a chaotic mess of papers and trash, and is your family life full of drama? Perhaps you can see how your energies reflect themselves throughout your life. You're never "one way" at work and "another way" at home—look closely, and you'll see that if you're living a split life, that division will be seen in everything you do.

When you're working with your home and environment, recognize that it occupies a significant place in the Flow. The physical objects you surround yourself with impact your own Flow, to varying degrees. So if you're having trouble making changes, or you want to support or increase new ones, take time to alter your home (or any other place you spend a lot of time in) to reflect your desires. If you work in a cubicle and want a job with freedom, then decorate the cubicle's walls with kites or images of planes, balloons, or birds—anything that acts as an "energy anchor" to push your thoughts and feelings toward feelings of freedom. Of course when you look at these images, it's important that you not feel longing or yearning; instead, feel joy, reach, ambition, or attainment.

One of the best times to see your environment clearly is after being away from it for a few days. The next time you get home from a trip, for instance, notice how you feel when you walk in the door (besides relief!). Let your eyes glance across your rooms and sense what feels wrong, dirty, old, or not like you. What isn't working? When you're home, you tend to attune yourself to your surroundings, but when you leave, you "detune." This is why you can find the freshest perspective the moment you walk back in the door.

If you need something new in your life, like a big change, then pack up lots of your old junk and put it in the garage or closet. Don't give it all away if you don't want to—just get it out of sight so there's more space in your home. Space creates opportunity, and that's what you want in your Flow. Much of this is common sense; just use your gut to make your surroundings match your manifesting.

Chapter 14

Look Through a New Lens

In this chapter, I look at a few beliefs I've developed as a manifesting practitioner that might be somewhat controversial. Over the years, my work with the Flow has led me to reinterpret—or replace—many beliefs I once held. Here are a few commonplace concepts that are recast in the light of Flowthinking.

The Presence of Evil

Early on in my practice of manifesting, I had a very simple epiphany: there is no evil. I was shown that it's really only a label for a broad array of conditions that cause suffering. *There is no evil; there is only that which causes suffering.*

You can look at anything from the perspective of "causing suffering" or "not causing suffering." When we do this, we can see how the term *evil* is selectively applied and loses much meaning, except as a way to label things that we're afraid of. It's far better to recognize fear as fear than to call it "evil."

When we identify those things that we're afraid of, we gain control over this powerful emotion and we reclaim our ability to shape our lives. However, when we label something as evil, we become powerless in the face of this "something else" and become a victim to it, passively acquiescing to it in our Flow.

If you look at how suffering is at the core of all supposed evil, you'll see that what you're really scared of is this potential to suffer or see others in anguish. Admittedly, I'm glossing over a profound subject here, but the idea is to simply start a conversation—*to restart your thinking*—about a potential restriction in your awareness that can affect your manifesting ability. When you're diminishing your energy by fearing evil, you're creating a self-imposed limitation and allowing yourself to give up your power. If you can reassess your understanding of evil and overcome your dread of it, then you've freed yourself from an emotional shackle that's kept you bound in your thinking.

There's no reason to be scared of evil, so you can let go of the fear that it will ever overpower or hurt you. *There is only suffering,* which is something that you can work to avoid. People both inflict suffering on others and participate in it themselves all the time, but suffering is not evil.

Let's take a look at a few examples and see how the difference between suffering and evil can be confusing depending on the perspective:

— When a person hurts a dog, he's indeed causing suffering, but is that evil? In countries where dogs are eaten, they're routinely slaughtered, and no one considers that evil. But in countries such as the United States, where they're considered our best friends, such an act is considered cruel if sufficient pain was inflicted on the animal. No matter what, the dog suffers, but our understanding and degree of empathy is what causes us to deem this evil or not.

— If someone kills another human being, they're causing suffering. Is that evil? When a country goes to war and happens to kill women and children, we call it "collateral damage." It's an unfortunate side effect, but we don't say that country is committing evil. However, when a country's citizens decide to slaughter one another in mass genocide, we absolutely call it the influence of evil.

When *anyone* is killed—be it through war, genocide, homicide, the death penalty, or something else—it always causes *suffering*. It's only our justification of the killing, or our disapproval of it, that causes us to label it evil or not.

— When a person fears demons, evil spirits, or the devil, are they fearing evil, or the potential to suffer at the hands of one of these scary things? When we fear an outside force, what we're really scared of is that this force will somehow hurt us or someone we love. But evil is not a force that emanates from an unholy darkness, and even if there *was* an unholy darkness of any kind, then all it can do is *cause the condition of suffering*. Agony, misery, fear—these are the darker colors on God's palette. And certain energy conditions do have the potential to be wellsprings for these energies. Riots, plagues, wars, famines, terror, wanton murder—each of these can generate huge quantities of suffering—and you can say the same about any "negative entities" you can conjure up in your imagination. But even the darkest demon you can dream up only has one ability: to cause suffering or even the illusion of "eternal suffering." But you, as a part of God, can always choose to have "had enough" and move away from it. You, as a filament of Source, are that powerful.

The Permanence of the Soul

When people fear evil, one of their biggest concerns is that their soul could be stolen or damaged. No soul can be stolen; neither can you obliterate a soul or make it cease to exist. Since all souls are equally of God or Source or Flow, stealing a soul would only mean moving it from one point to another. All "souls" are just containers for the cumulative data of our experience, which makes us into the "I" or self that we get to know. If you hit this "I" with a hammer, bombed it, or disintegrated it somehow, you'd merely be scattering this data, but it would remain. When something is known, from that point forward it's always known, no matter where it is or what shape it's in.

I take solace in this idea, because it reminds me that I can never be destroyed, absorbed, forgotten, or erased. Imagine a jar of beads as a human soul. If you drop the beads into a pool and swirl them around, they may have moved, but they're still there. Distance or cohesion is an illusion of perspective. Even if you crushed the beads into nothing but their molecular components, you'd remember that they were never more than their quantum parts anyway—they were just clinging together into the appearance of beads from your perspective.

Your soul is likewise indestructible. Remember, it's not some distinct, ghostlike thing. The soul is just a term for a vast collection of energy that's cohesively you and that spans many levels. And it will remain "you" for as long as God holds self-awareness—all of eternity.

Suffering Keeps It Interesting

You have so many variables to "keep it interesting" in this physical world that you wouldn't want everything planned and known in advance—what excitement or thrill is there in a roller coaster where every curve is predictable and known? There's no self-discovery possible unless new situations continually arise for you to interact with. Some of these new circumstances may encompass energies that you didn't specifically choose, in order for you to experience the surprise of your reaction. You must surprise yourself in order to get to know who you are. If you didn't offer new situations to your existence all the time, you'd always know your response and wouldn't get to know new parts of yourself.

So when you confront the shock of something that causes suffering, it's your choice as to how the encounter can proceed. Will you choose to immediately turn your attention away and begin Flowing—instead feeling happiness, ease, and comfort? Or will you allow fear and suffering the privilege of a response or engagement from you? And if so, will it be a reactive or a pre-active response?

Sometimes, if someone or something you care about is being harmed, you'll feel suffering no matter what. Being powerless in the face of their hurt is a form of suffering, so do all you can, physically and energetically, to alleviate their anguish. Move into your Flow and begin feeling how well the people you care about are doing, as well as how many new opportunities open for them to move out of their misery. Feel yourself lifted up, able to perceive how they're engaged in experiences that will soon pass. Contact them on an energy level and converse with them in the Flow. Respond to their suffering with the feelings and actions *you choose,* not the feelings you're *expected* to have (which often only perpetuate a bad situation).

Whenever we see suffering in our world, we can absolutely choose to alleviate it. Just because everyone has the power to be a self-directed manifester doesn't mean we can leave a baby in an abusive home or a child soldier fighting in a different part of the world. Use your Flow and your actions to bring relief to these situations and to allow children, animals, the elderly, the disabled, or anyone who has the "toughest" or most restrictive rules in this game, to have something better in their lives. If we work to create health, warmth, stability, and security in others' lives, we'll add these qualities to *all* our lives as these "substances" become more prevalent in our world's Flow.

The world doesn't have to be a hellish place—*we* have made it that way. We perpetuate our inequities and injustices through our inattention to our lives, our Flow, and our power as we run around seeking only to fulfill our most basic survival instincts.

So instead, let's give God something new to do: how about creating heaven on Earth? We haven't had that experience yet, but it's certainly possible for us to accomplish if we choose. Our problem is that we haven't globally agreed to do so yet. But by changing your thinking and reclaiming power over your life, you'll add at least one more person to the pool of self-aware beings here.

The Reality of Past Lives

In my line of work in the self-development world, I've had the opportunity to talk with, and get to personally know, many interesting teachers who are well-known leaders in the fields of spirituality and self-empowerment.

So when I found myself unwilling to accept one of the most common metaphysical dogmas (that of past lives), I began to ask myself, "Who am I to contradict old and venerable belief systems and such intelligent people?"

I think that many of us feel afraid to admit we might disagree with others. We're also inclined to assume that if something is old and respected, it has to be right . . . or there has to at least be *some* truth behind it. If we're told something that at face value seems right, we tend to accept it without much thought.

When I started to feel an unease with the idea of past lives, it was quite unsettling to me. As I pursued my research into the quantum nature of our universe, the idea of past lives (at least as we commonly understand them) began to unravel. I began to see the concept of time as something artificial and illusory, and the idea of past, present, and future lives became harder to believe in. I came to understand the idea that all time is essentially "now" in the quantum nature of reality. In our corporal world, time is just a law that merely lets the three dimensions of height, width, and depth exist as more than a still picture. Time allows those dimensions to move—we could not take a step without the time allowed for us to move our leg from *here* to *there*. Movement allows growth, and growth is an accumulation of experience, which is what we're here to do (along with deepening Source's understanding of Itself through these experiences)—so we need *time* as a way to do that.

But once we remove ourselves from the physical world (and the majority of our being is already existing beyond it), time becomes nonessential. There is no "here" or "there" to get to since it all becomes nonphysical data—flowing fields of information.

So when we discuss past lives, let's imagine for a moment what's happening before we're born. Here we can see if Source would really need to commit trillions of parts of Itself (you, me, and everyone else) to a "reincarnational ladder" of lifetimes through the slow, slogging method of time.

As FILAMENTS OF SOURCE, we're essentially receptacles for experience. Experience yields understanding and increased awareness of Self. If you were more than a filament of Source—*if you were all of Source Itself*—and wanted to absorb the most self-awareness you could, how would you do this? Remember that time is just a rule in a game that you create. It isn't real. So when you do something, it happens all at once. *The past, present, and future are all affected simultaneously.*

Now say that You, as Source, decide You want to know who You are. You understand that You'll need an objective observer—a pretend "something" outside Yourself to act as your mirror—but all You have to work with as materials is Yourself! So You decide to allow every aspect of Yourself to become engaged in games of self-discovery.

Thus, You open each of your marvelous bits of consciousness all at once into this thing called "time" that lets You feel as though You're experiencing small movements of perception, one after another. By feeling this "slowed down" sensation, You're able to see patterns emerge, and You can "watch" as all these filaments of Yourself appear to have sequential encounters—each yielding a tiny bit of delicious knowledge.

No matter how trivial or large each unit of experience is—whether You exist as an animal, vegetable, or mineral—it adds to the understanding of Yourself.

When one part of You, as a human, picks up a piece of litter off a beach, You have the feeling of muscles moving and a hint of satisfaction to tuck away. When another part of You says "I do" in a marriage ceremony, You have a feeling of overwhelming love and fulfillment—a peak experience to be treasured.

When one piece of You, as a dandelion, blows in the wind in a grassy field, Your tiny stem warmed with sunlight, You experience the simple satisfaction of warmth and the caress of breeze. When another bit of You is burning hot and bright in the core of a sun, exploding with fiery strength, You feel that, too.

All of You is engaged simultaneously across time (past, present and future) in an almost infinite number of forms—from rocks to dinosaurs to humanoids to alien life—to absorb the experience of Self.

Now, if all of You is engaged in these experiences *at once,* would You send parts of Yourself through them again and again? Why would you need to if *all* of You was already fully engaged? Effectively, You'd need to send a single piece of Your awareness into multiple time lines at the same time, and You'd have to allow each part of that original awareness to collect experience before it merged back into its natural whole, outside of time again. It's difficult to understand why You'd take just one bit of self-awareness and send it through this life game multiple times along a rigid ladder of past lives, each time wiping the memory of the life before, especially when You can just as easily send a fresh filament of Yourself to collect the experience firsthand without having the filter of multiple personalities to muffle the experience through. In some sense, living numerous lives in sequence means working from a limited palette because it suggests that there are only so many flecks of consciousness to go around, so they have to be recycled—yet God has no limit to Itself.

However, this is just speculation, because God is infinitely creative and there are many ways of doing things that are unknowable in our limited physical perspective. What I'm suggesting is that there's still a missing piece—a deeper understanding yet to be revealed—and that we should be cautious in accepting the "many lives" model, especially when it engenders so much baggage in terms of "learning" and "karma" or having to be graded on some kind of cosmic measuring scale. If we do live multiple lives, I have no doubt it's not for the reasons we now believe.

This being said, our consciousness does have the ability to move in and out of *other* people's lives, and our own consciousness may be engaged in certain experiences all at once, in effect living many lives, but not sequentially at all. Living "out of sequence" like this implies that there are never any "lessons" to carry through. All of us are just absorbing many experiences for our enrichment, having a fabulous time in the game. We get to be whomever we want and wherever we want, and we can suffer in one place (Earth) and be filled with unending joy in another (heaven) all at once.

Imagine a giant whose dipped each of his fingers into ten different lives all at once—that could be you, simultaneously absorbing experiences in ten time periods in ten parts of the world. The "giant" is the rest of you—your larger, collected consciousness—and your "fingers" are the individual personalities engaged in these lives.

I may in fact be in the body of a medieval woman, in the body of a young Persian boy, and in the body of a being in the far-distant future or on another planet. Other parts of me could be existing in realms of what we call "angels" or "spirit workers"; but this is all happening in the *now,* not in some linear succession of time where each life impacts one another.

Writing about the validity of past lives is difficult because I'm aware that there's more than one theory. Our nature is to always crave the black-and-white answer, but as you know, God loves variety and more than one path.

I've personally experienced past-life regressions that have felt real and profound. What I saw in these regressions even fit well with my personality and often matched or helped explain a situation in my life today. Perhaps what I've seen is just another part of me, having another simultaneous existence, and where I'm very similar to this other "me," our paths overlap or become blurred.

AS YOU READ THE MUSINGS ABOVE, you might also have wondered, "If the past, present, and future happen all at once, then isn't everything known already? Where is free will?"

A physicist will talk about reality as constant waves of potential that collapse into finite points of being from a pool of possible outcomes. Will you turn your car left or right? Will you answer the phone or let it ring? The moment—the now—represents each point of collapse or the point when the cosmos is etched with a particular data set describing how things are moment by moment. Until the specific instant, everything *is* a possible outcome. We're the catalysts for what becomes etched in the universe. We are the pens. But it's as if we etch into sand, because as quickly as the moment is had, it's gone. But the data is not lost. It's just stored—it's been collected and experienced. "Next!" says the universe.

So is there free will? *Yes!* And it coexists with the idea that everything is in a concurrent state of "becoming" and "became." This is perhaps one of the most difficult concepts to grasp, locked as we are within a time line. The fact is that God is both.

Chapter 15

Psychic Phenomena

Marine Maj. Charles Tinney was on a tour in Iraq in 2006 when a friendly German shepherd–collie mix wandered up to him. The dog had lost an ear and an eye, had terrible bite wounds, and had been hit with explosives—such is the unfortunate effect of war on animals.

Charles decided to care for this stray, but he was soon ordered back to his command post 80 miles away and was forced to leave this dog that he called "Bullseye" behind.

After two days, the dog managed to find Charles at his post, and the marine took it as sign that they were meant to be together. The story has a happy ending, with Bullseye later coming to the United States to live with Charles.

But the real story here is Bullseye's journey. How did a dog cross 80 miles of dirt and sand to locate this man who'd been good to him? He couldn't have just relied on scent since Charles wasn't marching on foot. How did this animal know which path would lead him through the desert? At the start of the journey, Bullseye had 360 potential different directions to choose from, with 359 leading away from Charles. Perhaps Bullseye watched the man leave and trailed his caravan—but is that possible at 20, 30, or even 60 miles per hour?

Was it blind luck? Or did Bullseye always have the "experience" of Charles as his end point, and he simply followed this feeling as one energy being to another?

While we don't often know the particulars, we do hear stories similar to this one all the time. Some dogs and even cats trek hundreds of miles between states looking for owners who've moved, showing up weeks and even months later. We try to find the logical answer—while sometimes there is one, in most instances, there's just no possible way that an animal could have tracked down its owner.

When I think of stories like these, I remember that all around us are countless examples of similarly strange situations. We tend to gloss them over, like we do reports of alien lights over major cities—we dismiss them as strange, freaky, and so unexplainable that we turn our heads away and simply refuse to deal with them . . . let alone consider their implications. I often joke that if aliens were really ever to come here, many of us would stubbornly refuse to acknowledge their existence, and not for any other reason than it's often easier to block out what we can't understand.

I believe that Bullseye identified himself with Charles, and when Charles left, Bullseye simply continued to "feel" him all the way to his physical location. As if following an invisible string through the woods, Bullseye chased the energy of his new friend until he reached him again.

Similar things happen to us when we make connections with other people and somehow follow them through time—often for years—before reconnecting again in the most unlikely places. The energy attachment never ceased; we just had things to do in the interim before being led to one another again.

We believe in magnetic guidance, we believe in radar tracking—there are so many methods we *have* identified that exist outside of human biological senses that it's pure arrogance to believe we have discovered them *all*. That we can track someone's energy signature through time and space isn't amazing to me at all; in the world of the Flow, this fits in perfectly.

Feeling Your Future Flow

I used to think that psychics were somehow special and unique. Telepathy, clairvoyance, clairsentience, and precognition—each was an exotic specialty that certain people seemed to have been born with a skill for. I encounter many people who feel this way, and I understand where this comes from. The aura of "magic" clings to people who are simply adept at reading the Flow. Individuals who are intuitive, no matter what their specialty is, have learned to use and pull information from the Flow to access data.

The Flow ties us all together. It's a vast repository for all the information you could ever want about anything—past, present, or potential future. If you can tap into the Flow, you'll find yourself right in the matrix of it all. It's like going on the Internet and then deciding just what kind of information you want to call up.

If you want to see into the future, allow your mind to drift forward in your Flow (rather than sending out information as you do when manifesting) in order to *receive* information. In other words, when you manifest, you're putting information *into* your Flow; when you're using your intuition or psychic sense, you're pulling information *out* of the Flow.

Let's say that you want to know if buying a certain house is a good idea. To find out, you'd enter your Flow, feel the essence of this home, and then pose the question. How bold or clear of an answer you receive depends on how skilled at this you are. If you've ever hit a golf ball, you know that your first few attempts sent the ball flying only a few feet. You had to practice a lot to hit better shots. Learning to see future outcomes in your Flow is very similar to this. You need to work at it. When you're told to listen to your intuition, you're being told to *practice* hearing what the energy is saying or doing.

Psychics who read the future are simply looking at potential "lines of destiny." In other words, they're looking at all the situations in various stages of manifestation in your life and sharing with you what they see. These people can tell you what's coming up by the "feeling" they receive from the situations that are being created in your Flow.

This is why precognitive psychics are often wrong—they're reading the *most probable* future based on all the information you've put into your Flow. It's like watching the trajectory of a marble as it rolls down a sloped board, and the psychic can tell you where it will probably go based on its current path. Your future actions will tend to reflect those of your past in almost every area, so you'll in fact encounter what they see. You'd have to really disrupt the trajectory of that marble (which is quite possible, through your focused Flowdreaming) in order to change its path.

For instance, if I'm feeling like I could use a vacation, then I've already put that feeling into my Flow. So if a psychic tells me that I'll be going to Europe, it validates the fact that I've begun manifesting the vacation, and forces are organizing this on my behalf. The psychic is simply sensing where the marble of my intention is rolling to.

Since you're manifesting every minute, you could also make a decision in the next few days that skews this "most likely" line of destiny in a totally different direction. Maybe after the psychic said that you'll be traveling to Europe, you instead thought, *No, if I'm going to go anywhere, I want to see Japan.*

There—you've altered the future, and that "Europe Flow" is like a grape withering on the vine. A new bud blooms instead: Japan. Thus, the prediction doesn't come true (or maybe it's only partially true).

What can you make of predictions for things you don't see or haven't felt at all? Recall that other people's Flows have as much impact on your life as your own. Psychics aren't just looking at you; they're looking at the energy swarm of everyone and everything that surrounds you—your family, friends, and co-workers—and picking out the threads of events that seem like they're "near" you. So if a psychic says that you'll be changing careers, she may be feeling the unease of the company you work for, since companies also send out energy waves into the Flow, and your employer's Flow is entwined with your own. Even though something like this could be a shock to you, it was really already in place in your Flow.

Mediumship and Channeling

What about other kinds of phenomena, such as mediums who can reach across life to speak with the dead? A medium is just talking to a consciousness that's not in a body. You already know that your mind—in fact, the greater part of you—exists outside of your physical self as a quantum field of information. A medium can feel for the energy or consciousness of whomever you want to reach, or he can be open to someone who wants to reach you, relaying the information to you from this other energy Flow. (Although I've explained a medium's function very simply, it does require practice and some natural talent, just as with any art or sport.)

And what of channelers, or people who speak with spirits and other forms of energy? (Again, you know I only use the word *spirit* since it's familiar to us.) In reality, this person is just accessing another form of consciousness that we don't think of as human. Perhaps this other awareness or bit of "God's perception" has *never been* human. Because of this, you hear from perspectives that seem much deeper and wiser than your own.

I'm reminded of when my mother first began speaking to the Beings*. We were sitting in the living room of her house chatting about some mundane topic, and as I happened to glance over to the dining room, I was shocked to "see" a being in a white robe sitting there. Not really *there,* but there in essence, like seeing an image reflected in a pair of eyeglasses. More powerful than the image was the communication that accompanied it. I felt/saw/heard

---

*To read transcripts or hear audio samples of the Beings' communication, visit **www.VenusAndrecht.com**.

that this was *a really wise being*. When I told my mother, we were both completely puzzled by what this meant. I've only seen apparitions maybe half a dozen times, and only when there's been a strong message to relay.

Not long after, my cousin drowned in an accident and my mother went through horrible grief. As a result, she began communicating with the very same group of energies that had shown themselves to me as that apparition. I had seen an energy consciousness already present in her Flow, that would only reveal itself after certain events that would trigger what has since become a lengthy communication with them.

Once she began conversing with these Beings, I found that, oddly, they were accessible to me at any time, too. I hadn't sought them out, but there they were. When I asked why I could also "hear" and converse with them, I was told that both my mother's energy and my own were so similar that once they "attuned" themselves to her, I was also tuned in by default. It was a very odd feeling, and she and I had many conversations together about whether one or both of us was cracking up and slipping into loopy land.

I suspect that many of us are in conversation with other energies, first and foremost our own Greater Self, but not often in such a spectacular way. Many of us have also felt what we might describe as God speaking to us, answering us, or offering us solace, and then we wondered if it truly happened or if we were just making it up.

Eventually, I figured that since the information I was receiving was so valuable to me, it didn't matter who or where it was coming from. I have no need to convince anyone else, and neither should you.

YOU CAN PURSUE ANY OF THESE other ways of working with your Flow that I've glossed over here. You might try precognition, mediumship, or channeling—or even just learning to better hear your own intuitive voice. Follow whatever path of learning speaks to you. I've found that there are many teachers with wonderful educational programs, and usually we end up taking a bit from several of them as we find our own eventual way of doing things.

But place their teachings in the context of your Flow (even if your teacher is unaware of this concept). When you can practice your intuitive or telepathic skills from within your Flow, or recognize them as just another aspect of your Flow, you can take advantage of the full scope of the Flow's power to support these new skills.

My own experience is that whenever I Flowdream, I often encounter a flood of strong intuitive feelings about very short-term events—as in 24 to 72 hours away. I'm not looking for this, it's just that since I'm so used to going in to the Flow to program my future, I sometimes wind up "viewing" my near future as well. The feeling I get is of the events "hanging over my head," along with a surge of understanding about things that are very, very close to me.

Don't expect to get this yourself, as we all experience different sensations and cues. But you have great capacity to learn how to receive within your Flow. Remember, most so-called psychic skills are just the counterpoint to manifesting in your Flow. One skill set receives data, and the other sends it. You may do one or both.

Chapter 16

Take Back Your Power

As you begin practicing Flowdreaming, you'll find yourself thinking more about power and responsibility. On the one hand, you'll recognize that you're a powerful creator seeking to enrich your life with whatever strikes your fancy, but on the other, you understand that you have a responsibility to others and to the world. How is this reconciled? When do you become downright *selfish* in your pursuit of happiness? And does manifesting give you permission to hurt others, since you presume they have the power to stop you and simply choose not to?

Although Source *allows* suffering, it doesn't mean it *should* be perpetuated. Likewise, just because people *can* Flow away from harm doesn't mean that they *will* or even know that it's possible to do so.

A conscious manifester takes on a huge responsibility because the world you create for yourself becomes part of the greater world around you. Your life is part of the world's life. If you create bounty for yourself but your actions harm someone else, then you've also created misery. Is that who you are, or who you want to be? We have a responsibility to create with a larger perspective than just pleasing ourselves. When I choose to recycle, for instance, I'm not doing it for *me*. I'm doing it for my kids' lives 20 years from now. When I choose to walk rather than take the car out, I'm not doing it just for my health, I'm doing it so that a tiny frog in a lake somewhere can enjoy a few more years of existence before its species winks out of existence. When I send money to a group helping refugees, I'm not doing it for me, I'm doing it because that stain of human misery seeps into the Flow and creates a haze of despair that colors the energies of our whole world, and depresses all of our opportunities.

The Power in My Beliefs

I recently had a very important interview with a man who was writing an article about my company for a highly respected magazine. I was prepared to talk about my job, my own accomplishments, the success of the company, and the wonderful capabilities of my employees. I wasn't prepared to talk about the Flow or my personal philosophy . . . and so, of course, this was the first thing he asked me about.

He asked me the classic question that all scholars ask about the art of manifesting, which goes something like this: "Do you think that a person who's poor, in a bad situation, ill, or abused created or manifested this suffering for themselves? In other words, aren't you blaming the victim?"

When a really horrible atrocity occurs, it's unthinkable to blame the victims. For someone to say that people would intentionally create devastation for themselves reveals a mind that can only think in black and white. Victims *may* have created their horror as a result of prior thoughts and actions, or they might have been unknowingly swept into a Flow of events and become caught up in a collective experience. Or, life could have dealt them a complete surprise (cancer, car wrecks, and so on), with the caveat, "See what you can do with this: get to know yourself/God through this encounter."

Almost all tragedies have more than one participant. There are those who perpetrate the atrocity, those who are harmed by it, and those who fail to prevent it.

When we see suffering, it's our choice as to how we respond. We can choose to *prevent, alleviate,* or *cause* pain; or we can *allow* it by looking the other way. What you choose to do or not do will affect you and your Flow. You can see that this leads to a strong sense of stewardship in a person who lives with the Flow philosophy. I often joke that I'm a *real* conservative. I want to *conserve* our natural resources by building healthful energy sources. I want to *conserve* our wealth by educating our children to continue our great society responsibly and in a caring way. I want to conserve—to *preserve*—our freedom by agitating for the ability to resist, to think and believe how we want, and to prevent unwarranted breaches of our privacy. Most of all, I want to be a steward of life, so that our earth remains pure, our land remains home for the many species here, and our society remains rich with freedoms and liberties unheard of in history past. As an onlooker to most situations, I feel it's my duty to say what is acceptable and what isn't, and to change my behavior and participation to reflect my feelings whenever I can so I can support all these goals with not just my feelings, but my actions. Both sides of the coin.

I WAS DEEPLY DISTURBED BY my lack of agility in answering the aforementioned reporter that day. I stuttered, flubbed around, and made lame efforts to explain the Flow as if I hadn't spent a decade practicing and teaching it. I even joked that I had no sound bite ready, and that the question he asked me is usually part of a long conversation that leads into new and interesting insights for me each time I have it.

The best answer I currently had was that there *is* no clear-cut answer. "We can become victims by choice, or by default. Our lives are always up for play: sometimes we program the outcome, but other times we see what interesting hand we're dealt," I told him. "It's a game. We come here to explore ourselves and to see what we're made of. How could we do that if we knew every card ahead of time? It would be a dull game if we always knew what was coming and who was going to win. Manifesting means steering the game in your favor—not controlling it—like a dancer leads his partner as opposed to moving her arms and legs for her."

On my way home from the interview, I realized that besides trying to trip me up with the classic "How can you blame the victim" questions, he really just wanted to see how true I was to my own convictions.

Even as I was speaking to him, I thought, *How could I possibly tell the whole of it to this guy in a half-hour interview? How could I lay out the specifics of my philosophy without sounding like a New Age kook, or even a kook who happens to rebel against most other New Age orthodoxy?*

I realized that I probably feel like you, or the many people who call my radio show or write me and say, "My family thinks I'm nuts. What do I tell them?"

I usually say, "Why do you care? Who cares if your brother-in-law is born-again and thinks you're going to hell? Or if your sister the doctor looks down on your spirituality? Why does it matter?" But it does. I wanted to seem like I had all the answers. I wanted to win him over and feel his approval so that it would validate my own beliefs. If this intelligent man could agree with me, then by golly I *was* right.

Later, while showering and thinking about my day in the quiet space between dinnertime and putting the kids to bed, I realized that people call my talk show all the time for an answer that will make them feel like the weight is lifted off their shoulders. Callers want someone to tell them what's actually true, just like I wanted to tell the reporter what was true, but I could only tell him what was true for *me*. I just couldn't stop thinking, *Is that good enough?*

Take Back Your Power

All of life is an exchange of ideas and beliefs. In the U.S., the idea of free will and the potential to organize one's life in the moment—with the incredible power it offers—is a valuable idea. Yet I've come to see that our desire for self-empowerment is universal.

Recently, a man from Pakistan who wanted to learn to Flowdream e-mailed me. While I was surprised that someone in Pakistan had found me, I was not surprised about the desire. I have received e-mails and spoken to people all over the world, from Japan to Bahrain, Norway, Mexico, and India—too many places to name. I've heard from our deployed soldiers in Iraq and Afghanistan, professors at elite universities and government labs who were afraid to let anyone else know that they're even interested in the topic of manifesting, and hundreds of other folks—people who share the simple desire to figure out what else they can do to empower themselves now that they've exhausted all that physical life has to offer.

The desire to take back our power over our lives and the inner knowing that this is in fact possible throbs in each of us. I frequently receive correspondence from men and women who state, "I've always done this. I've always felt this place of power—what you call the Flow—but I just never knew it had a name."

To borrow a phrase from Eckhart Tolle, when you access "the power of now" and focus on the moment at hand, it's like quieting yourself to hear your heartbeat. You hear the pulse of your Flow as you begin to listen for the cycles in your life: beat, rest, beat, rest.

The names we give the Flow are arbitrary. I call it "the Flow" because that makes sense to me—it seems to describe some fundamental quality of Source. But no matter what we call this force, the constant is the forward-feeling motion or the surge of life energy that carries us into our futures.

Other cultures will surely see the Flow within the context of their own heritage. Will someone from Asia recognize it as chi or prana? Scientists may call it the zero-point field or something similar. Christians may understand it as God, and being within it is like being submerged in God's river of light.

Through time, people who practiced the art of manifesting have always been with us. Our ancestors labeled them oracles, prophets, shamans, witches, sorcerers, alchemists, or healers. Certain people have always felt the heartbeat of energy in our lives a little more acutely than others, and it's no accident that we've had these psychics, healers, and energy workers forever. Each has accessed this deep well-spring of energy within the bounds of his or her cultural understanding. And the access has been universal—every culture has recognized this place and this state of energy.

That you've picked up this book means you've joined this group of seekers and now carry on the tradition yourself.

Why It's So Good to Be Wrong

Even as I continue to work with the energies of the universe more and more, I realize that there's still so much I don't know. We're all travelers at the *beginning* of the road. Think on this—how many miracles have you *truly* seen? (I sometimes joke that if we were all really on our "last lives," I'd expect to see a lot more miracles being done around this place with all these enlightened beings walking around.)

I don't exempt myself from this criticism. Even all the truths and speculations I'm sharing with you are a jumble of prescient insights coupled with "feelings"—some of which continue to change. I'm happy that my beliefs are in a constant state of change, because change shows me how my sense of self-knowledge is continually expanding. I'll be happier if, five years from now, I'll be able to update everything I've written here with still more insights and new observations to both complement and challenge what I'm presenting now.

This may make you feel a little uncomfortable. Being told that you're only learning *a* truth—or a *current* truth—as opposed to *the Truth,* is unsettling. But what if the absolute truth is in a state of becoming and not fixed at all? Surely the truth about everything isn't already dead, inflexible, and unchanging.

My experience is that we always want someone else to tell us what the truth is, because then we're relieved of the experience of observing it for ourselves. (If there's a messiah, prophet, guru, channeled spirit, or anyone else who could give us the whole truth, I'm pretty sure that person would add, "This is only true for *me*.") All of my encounters with deeper energies have largely agreed on this point: some things are still in a state of becoming, and truth is part of that.

Many experiences have taught me never to blindly follow a teacher or guru, because then you follow the individual as well. We *all* have a connection to what we call Source or the divine. Some spiritual teachers have a more open, or stronger connection, and are able to communicate their understanding of it well to others, but there's always a part of them that's very human and contains the same flaws that you yourself have. Instead, follow the teachers' perspective. *Look where they're looking. See what they're seeing.* Retain your identity and uniqueness of thought as you look *with* them, not *at* them. I can't stress that enough.

Preachers, politicians, spiritual masters, and anyone who leads others can become trapped in their own garments, so to speak. *So look where they're looking*—they've probably found a glittering truth to behold, but you need to look past the human beings themselves to see it.

I handwrote a sign that I hung on my office wall for many years that said, A LITTLE DOUBT IS A GOOD THING, BECAUSE IT REMINDS YOU THAT YOUR MIND IS STILL OPEN. Anytime someone tells me definitively, "This is how it all works, and if you'd only adhere to what I teach, you'd win the lottery, retire, and never catch as much as a sniffle again," this is what I think: *Maybe that's your truth, but God is a building with 1,000 doors. What you're suggesting may be the path that does this for you, but I'm here to discover my own set of experiences, working with tools I'm still discovering. We did not come here to be the same. My job is to encounter an aspect of creation that is unlike anyone else's.*

The more I grow as a teacher, the more of a student I become, because *I learn what questions to ask.* The questions I asked when I was younger show me trolling through much shallower depths. As I learn and master more, I still find deeper soil to dig, where the complexities become greater and the answers are less easily discovered. That is how I know I'm in the realm of creation, in a place of great depth and potential.

Where Are We All Going?

Recently, I was reading about a man who's a devout atheist. He doesn't believe in a higher power because he simply can't believe in a "top-down" creator who would purposely design all of existence. It seems much more scientifically likely to him that life evolved upward, haphazardly, into its current state of complexity—the "bottom-up" view of creation.

Years ago in a sociology class, I learned a fascinating fact about how trends form. The example was fashion. Each year, the fashion world comes together to decide what the upcoming seasons will look like. (Haven't you ever wondered why so many stores and brands all offer the same colors and styles in the same season?) When these large stores and designers come up with the "look" and begin manufacturing mass amounts of clothes to conform to this look, it's called "top-down design." The rest of us are then told what's in style and what to wear.

On the other hand, teenagers and musicians are always rebelling against the current norms—often through fashion. Punks in the 1970s began ripping their clothes and safety pinning them back together. The new-wave look in the 1980s featured jeans bleached at home with holes cut in the knees. And, rappers in the 1990s started to wear their pants low and oversized. In every case, the bottom-up fashion of these movements drove the brass at the stores to begin tailoring their clothes to the street trends that were dictating the current hip fashions.

What we see, then, is a mix of both top-down and bottom-up trends driving the fashion world forward. The two propellants work off of one another, always using the other as a catalyst to either imitate or rebel against, while both dance together in the forward evolution of style. The "intelligent design" of the smart company executives and the bottom-up impact of small groups in the streets, clubs, and schools work together.

I sometimes wonder if we are doing something similar in our spiritual lives. We direct ourselves from "above," from the deeper consciousness that we are, yet we also contribute from the physical, human aspect that is our "street-level" self. Together we progress, absorbing experiences and gaining awareness. And if we do this as individuals, wouldn't it mean that as a group, all of Source Itself is likewise in a blossoming of self-exploration, guided through both an overarching awareness as well as through its countless component parts?

The ocean is made up of countless individual water molecules, but it simultaneously exists as a whole and acts uniformly to form waves and currents of extraordinary power that drive the weather patterns of our planet. Does each individual molecule drive the collective power of the ocean, or does the combined, overarching force of the ocean drive the molecules?

The "intelligent-design model" too often falls victim to the idea that some profound intelligence has planned everything—every speck of sand in the desert and every minute details of our own lives—and now watches to see how we'll do within our carefully planned cage. It causes us to suffer and has the power to relieve this suffering, and it has certain goals and plans for us and feels disappointment when we fail to reach them.

The "evolution-only model," on the other hand, suggests that no external or deeper sources are in play—we're simply accidents of nature living short, essentially meaningless lives, with reproduction our only true driving force. Consciousness and self-awareness are accidental by-products of evolution, and are a curious anomaly that may not even be particularly useful.

I think that most of us believe something in the middle of these two extremes. Certainly, Flowthinking has opened me to an understanding of a means in which both views complement each other. As a focused pinpoint of consciousness, each of us is a point of absorption, both independent and powerfully self-initiating, and still dependent on the larger consensual reality (the ocean) for our very existence. We're both a piece of the mind of God as well as continually creating that mind as we move along.

We're creatures of extraordinary power, and this power is active in every moment of our lives.

Chapter 17

Oh, and One Last Thing

Does our thinking *always* create our reality? The optimist in me wants to enthusiastically yell, "Yes!" There's nothing we like so much as a clear-cut, black-and-white rule that makes us feel *in control* and gives us a sense of comfort. We also like it better when someone tells us what to do, tells us what's right, and tells us what will happen—if we'd only adhere to certain dogma. Some of the most popular books ever written, from the Bible to *How to Catch a Man,* adhere to this principle of laying down surefire rules for success: you'll succeed if only you follow *x, y,* and *z.* In the self-development world, I see evidence of this all the time: *people want to be told what will fix them and exactly how to do it.*

I can relate completely, because when another person has the answer, then all the guessing and self-doubt disappears. Also, if a situation doesn't work out and you did everything that person said, you've got someone other than yourself to blame. If you hear that you can just think everything in and out of existence, I can understand how you'd really want this to be true—for everything.

Lately, we've truly seen a crescendo of interest in this idea that our thoughts create our reality. As already noted, this idea is far from new—it's ancient—but every so often it gets pulled from the dustbin of time and resurrected for a new audience. The thing is, it used to be so easy for critics to discredit it, pushing the idea back under the rug for another few decades or centuries. But today we're finally developing tools that allow us to test this theory. The idea of manifesting is no longer only acknowledged by religion and spirituality. Well-respected scientists are seeing remarkable evidence that our thoughts really can affect physical things—as in, you think it, and it happens.

Of course, the next thing we want to do is rally and cry out, "See, we told you so!" Except that it doesn't seem to work *every* time. There seem to be other factors—limiters—that can put the brakes on or skew the results. We know a little, it seems, but we don't know it all. I've found these limiters in the form of glass ceilings, in the "rules of game," in my body, the environment, history, my old beliefs, my default mode, that random bit of chaos in my life, and my plain old negative thinking.

So, YOU MAY STILL BE WONDERING, *when does manifesting work, and when doesn't it?*

First, you have to take in to account the series of limiting factors—"your rules"—that define the general sketch of your life. You're born when the planets are exerting a certain energetic impact on your individual existence.

232

Your family will offer you a certain kind of early social-izing, define your economic comfort zone, and either love or harm you. And, you'll be born into a town or city in a country that exerts a cultural influence on you that helps shape your expectations for life. All of this creates your par-ticular focus (your unique lens) in the piece of Source, *you,* that has manifested Itself into reality. Each piece (person) is different because it wants to have its own unique set of experiences.

So there you are, an artist already set up with all the colors and tools for you to create with in your artist's bag. What will you do with them? What *can* you do with them?

Like a pinball shot in a pinball machine, you'll encoun-ter certain common elements in life. It's part of the expe-rience. The where, when, how, and to what degree are all negotiable. You can't know or precisely plan everything. If you could, then what would be the point of having the experience? You go to a movie to be entertained and an amusement park to be thrilled: you go through life to be excited, scared, amused, loved, and hated—and to see just what you're made of.

As a culture, we've made the mistake of falling deep into the idea that everything just happens to us, and that we're victims at every turn. We've failed to balance our intake of life so that it's sometimes new, unexpected, and exciting, while other parts are smooth, planned, and fore-seen. When you begin to manifest, you'll start to see a life that's impacted by your thinking in ways that can seem magical, because you've opened the door to a whole new level of ordering and arranging it.

In my own life, I've gradually seen more pleasurable and comfortable circumstances begin to appear, since this is fundamentally what I choose to create. I've been continually refining my default mode for a number of years. I couldn't close my eyes and think myself into winning a Pulitzer prize, growing a third kidney, or causing my house to build a second floor on top of itself. But I can choose to follow the path of ease in my Flow and program my desire for a happy home, wonderful work, lots of free time, healthy children, and a happy marriage. I can, and do, allow these desires to consume me and go out and attract situations that support these feelings. Life organizes itself around me in ways that sometimes seem like wildly exciting bonanzas that seem to drop from thin air, but more often it organizes itself in subtle, ongoing ways.

What I achieve through creative Flowdreaming far surpasses anything that I can achieve without it. With it, I'm a gambler sidling up to a game fixed in my favor. I'm an insider trader. I've fixed the bets. My default mode increases in complexity and precision every day, gradually disallowing all those bad situations I used to experience and letting in more of the profound experiences I've programmed it to give me. My Greater Self can stretch her hypothetical wings and bring me all kinds of things I would have otherwise blocked or ignored. She knows my emotional endgame, what I'm craving, and how to best find the physical complement to that desire.

This doesn't prevent tragedy from happening to me. Life is exciting; I anticipate an element of chaos, and I'm here to encounter everything I can. I'm just stepping up and taking the wheel, although the road itself is still full of unexpected potholes.

Above all else, the peace of mind that the practice of Flowdreaming creates for me is staggering. No matter what comes to me, I realize that I have a tool with which I can nudge things onto a track more to my liking. I won't fall off any path. I won't have to forever seek my life purpose. I'm never going to be graded or judged by anyone but my fellow humans and the people who love me. All this is such a relief to me. Each time I think of the Flow, I feel such a lightness of being.

When I look ahead, I see many avenues in various stages of completion, each leading to a new and exciting experience. If I dislike any road I begin to walk down, my Flow will help reorient me back to one that's more to my liking. It's that easy.

So, to answer the question, "Does our thinking *always* create our reality?"

I say, "Yes . . . and no."

Now, as you go forth to manifest, what will *you* choose to bring in?

Further Exploration

If you're interested in learning more about manifestation, and Flowdreaming in particular, please visit my Website: **www.Flowdreaming.com**. Here you can find free articles and MP3s, as well as links to discussion groups and other resources in which people share their experiences with the Flow. I hold workshops and occasionally do private consultations, and I've also developed a library of materials to teach you Flowdreaming using a series of CDs that's available in the Website store. And I always love to hear how Flowdreaming has helped you in your own life. E-mail me your own story anytime at **summer@flowdreaming.com**.

You might also enjoy visiting **www.GodIsAlwaysHappy. com**, Venus Andrecht's Website. Much of what you've read in this book found, if not its genesis, then its fine-tuning through the conversations between Venus, myself, and the Beings. You can find this extraordinary dialogue at her Website, both in written and audio form.

Emotional States and Their Uses

This table shows you all the resources found in your emotional tool box. Choose several of these emotions to pre-act into your Flow when Flowdreaming.

Being thankful	The feeling of thankfulness says, "My prayers have been answered." This is one of the most powerful phrases or feelings you can use. It implies that what you've asked for has already occurred, that you were deserving of it, and that you trust in the Flow and the deeper energies to provide for you.
Being deserving	This opens you to receiving all good things. Feeling deserving tells the Flow, "Yes! I am good enough for this! I will do wonderful things with this opportunity!" It's a highly productive emotion in the Flow.
Being acknowledged/ recognized/ rewarded	This feeling allows recognition and acknowledgment to flow your way and creates a feeling of you as a professional or luminary in your field. It opens new opportunities to move up and be seen and draws in respect for you and your ideas. In relationships, it opens an energy state that allows your partner to see your contribution and give you credit.
Being curious	This emotion opens you to the unknown and allows in new possibilities for success. You are stating that you don't know the best route, but your curiosity means that you'll accept it when it arrives.
Being trusting	This emotion creates room for the Flow to provide the best solution to your problem or the best way to implement your desire. It says that you have faith and are allowing the ideal circumstances to develop.

Being elevated	Being elevated or "lifted up" helps move you within your Flow to a new level. It's a good emotional tool to use when you feel that you've grown out of your current situation and need to move on to bigger horizons. This feeling helps grow a business, lifts you from years of inaction or stagnation, and puts you on a new road.
Being appreciated	This emotion means that you'll be rewarded for your efforts and moved into a higher place—taken to a new plateau. It's effective when seeking a new career or respect and admiration from someone. Similar to being acknowledged, this emotion sets up circumstances where you'll be respected, seen, and rewarded for your efforts. It's especially good for those who always feel like they "toil in vain," doing all the hard work but are never thanked for it.
Being wanted	This feeling can be used when working with relationships or in business. Being wanted means that someone sees something important in you, your products, or your services. It's a good emotion to use when seeking a new job or career.
Being desired	Similar to feeling wanted, feeling desired also helps create an aura of attraction around you; however, feeling desired generates more sensual overtones. You feel gorgeous, handsome, attractive, or desirable. Partners or friends are attracted to your potential wherever you go.

Being a radiant beacon	This feeling generates a strong sense of you as a focal point—where people or situations gather around. It's a great emotional tool for anyone who is seeking to draw in something, whether it be clients, lovers, or others. A radiant beacon is like a light in the dark.
Being healthy	This feeling washes you in vibrant health. It is auto-correcting, meaning that any effective resource of help will be drawn to you. Feeling yourself in a perfect state of health aligns your physical self with your deeper-energy self to create situations and conditions that support your ideal weight and fitness. When sick or recovering from an illness, feeling healthy programs your body's energy template toward vitality again.
Being magnetic	This feeling generates a strong attraction in the Flow. When you sense yourself pre-acting toward your desired wish, you can follow this with a feeling of being a radiant magnet, drawing in all the situations and future conditions that align themselves to the quality of your desire.
Being loved	This emotion acknowledges that you are both loved and lovable, and that this feeling surrounds you.
Sending love	Sending love outward while Flowdreaming fills your Flow with joy and happiness and imbues all your desires with harmony and great fulfillment. Situations that bring you more joy and love will begin arriving in response to these feelings.

Being full/ satisfied	This emotion suggests that you have enough of what you need, and are in perfect balance with this aspect of your life.
Being confident/ strong	Feeling strong, capable, and confident tells your Flow that you are ready for any matching situation where you can show leadership and initiative. It says, "Not only is this thing I'm feeling confident about here with me now, but I'm fully capable of keeping it in my life."
Being unstoppable	This feeling shows you as an icebreaker, moving ahead through circumstances that easily give way to your mighty strength. Nothing can obstruct you.
Being paced	This regulates the pace and flow of your life, especially helping with stressful situations. Feeling paced acknowledges that your future is both full and satisfying without being hectic.
Being calm/ at peace	This feeling creates balance and depth in stressful situations. It brings in opportunities for quiet time and helps you attain balance in your life.
Being freed	This emotion says, "I have the world at my feet!" It's especially good if you're leaving an abusive situation, a workplace that doesn't recognize your talents, or a relationship that no longer serves you. It moves the energies forward, away from stagnation.

Being safe/ shielded	This feeling creates havens of safety for you. It's a good emotion to use when you're insecure, shaky, worried, or in doubt about your future. A feeling of safety means that you're taken care of and shielded from any harm.
Being open	This emotion allows in new, unseen opportunities to come to you. It means that you're receptive to what the Flow brings.
Being aware	Feeling aware opens you to hearing, sensing, or otherwise understanding things that were obscured to you. It means that penetrating insights and situations will appear that allow you to see things more clearly.
Being alone	This sensation is useful when you're disengaging yourself from someone or something. Feeling alone or withdrawn is a way to make yourself disconnect from another person's Flow.
Being helped	This allows abundant opportunities to flood in that will help you achieve your goal. Whatever you need is supplied or drawn to you through the generous help of others.
Being excited/ anticipatory	This is an acknowledging feeling that states, "I know this will happen because I'm so excited about it!" It negates doubt.
Pulling close	A variation on feeling magnetic, a feeling of pulling something close helps speed the development of your desire.

Claiming ownership	A sensation of *This is mine* shows that what you ask for has already been delivered. It solidifies your desire and makes it real.
Being proud	Feeling pride is another emotion that solidifies the reality of your desire. It accentuates the feeling of your wish already having come true, and shows your resultant pride in what you created.
Being joyful	Joy is one of the best emotions for manifesting because sending waves of joy into your Flow both acknowledges that what you desire has come true and that the result of this is pure, unadulterated happiness.
Looking back	This feeling helps you sense that what you ask for is easily obtainable. It shows you how you might see your desire from the perspective of your future self after what you asked for already came true. It moves you out of any tendency to send feelings of "wishing" or "hoping" since it shows you far past the point of when your dream came to fruition.
Feeling release	A feeling of letting go or releasing is mandatory whenever you want to move away from negative feelings or resistance. You can visualize "letting go" like letting a billowing cape fly free from you and float away in your Flow. Feel a sensation of all your anxiety, worry, and self-doubt swirling out of you and falling away behind you into your Flow's past.

About the Author

Summer McStravick, the creator of Flowdreaming, has developed her knowledge of manifesting and the Flow into a series of free articles, CDs, books, and intimate workshops found at her Website, **Flowdreaming.com**.

She is also the network director of **HayHouseRadio. com**, an Internet-radio Website with a worldwide audience, where she's had the pleasure of hosting her own radio program entitled *Flowdreaming,* and co-hosting a weekly show with Dr. Wayne Dyer that has gone on to national exposure on XM Satellite Radio.

In her capacity as director of audio, radio, and new media at Hay House, Summer has enjoyed producing programs by and for the likes of Louise Hay, Jerry and Esther Hicks (Abraham), Suze Orman, Dr. Christiane Northrup, Dr. Wayne Dyer, Marianne Williamson, Doreen Virtue, and many other leaders in the fields of self-help and spirituality.

Summer lives with her husband and two children in Southern California.

HAY HOUSE TITLES OF RELATED INTEREST

YOU CAN HEAL YOUR LIFE, the movie,
starring Louise L. Hay & Friends
(available as a 1-DVD program and
an expanded 2-DVD set)
Watch the trailer at: **www.LouiseHayMovie.com**

THE SHIFT, the movie, starring Dr. Wayne W. Dyer
(available as a 1-DVD program and an expanded 2-DVD set)
Watch the trailer at: **www.DyerMovie.com**

---

*COURAGEOUS DREAMING: How Shamans Dream
the World into Being,* by Alberto Villoldo, Ph.D.

EVERYTHING YOU NEED TO KNOW TO FEEL GO(O)D,
by Candace Pert, Ph.D.

*IT'S THE THOUGHT THAT COUNTS: Why Mind Over
Matter Really Works,* by David R. Hamilton, Ph.D.

*THE LAW OF ATTRACTION:
The Basics of the Teachings of Abraham®,*
by Esther and Jerry Hicks

*THE POWER OF INTENTION: Learning to Co-create
Your World Your Way,* by Dr. Wayne W. Dyer

*SECRETS OF SUCCESS: The Science and Spirit of Real
Prosperity,* by Sandra Anne Taylor

*THE SPONTANEOUS HEALING OF BELIEF: Shattering
the Paradigm of False Limits,* by Gregg Braden

All of the above are available at your local bookstore,
or may be ordered by contacting Hay House (see next page).

We hope you enjoyed this Hay House book. If you'd like to receive a free catalog featuring additional Hay House books and products, or if you'd like information about the Hay Foundation, please contact:

Hay House, Inc.
P.O. Box 5100
Carlsbad, CA 92018-5100

(760) 431-7695 or (800) 654-5126
(760) 431-6948 (fax) or (800) 650-5115 (fax)
www.hayhouse.com® • www.hayfoundation.org

Published and distributed in Australia by:
Hay House Australia Pty. Ltd., 18/36 Ralph St., Alexandria NSW 2015
Phone: 612-9669-4299 • *Fax:* 612-9669-4144 • www.hayhouse.com.au

Published and distributed in the United Kingdom by:
Hay House UK, Ltd., 292B Kensal Rd., London W10 5BE
Phone: 44-20-8962-1230 • *Fax:* 44-20-8962-1239 • www.hayhouse.co.uk

Published and distributed in the Republic of South Africa by:
Hay House SA (Pty), Ltd., P.O. Box 990, Witkoppen 2068
Phone/Fax: 27-11-467-8904 • orders@psdprom.co.za • www.hayhouse.co.za

Published in India by: Hay House Publishers India, Muskaan Complex,
Plot No. 3, B-2, Vasant Kunj, New Delhi 110 070 • *Phone:*
91-11-4176-1620 • *Fax:* 91-11-4176-1630 • www.hayhouse.co.in

Distributed in Canada by: Raincoast, 9050 Shaughnessy St.,
Vancouver, B.C. V6P 6E5 • *Phone:* (604) 323-7100
Fax: (604) 323-2600 • www.raincoast.com

Tune in to **HayHouseRadio.com®** for the best in inspirational talk radio featuring top Hay House authors! And, sign up via the Hay House USA Website to receive the Hay House online newsletter and stay informed about what's going on with your favorite authors. You'll receive bimonthly announcements about Discounts and Offers, Special Events, Product Highlights, Free Excerpts, Giveaways, and more!
www.hayhouse.com®